A History Of The Singer Building Construction

A HISTORY OF
THE SINGER BUILDING
CONSTRUCTION

ITS PROGRESS FROM FOUNDATION TO

FLAG POLE

Edited by O. F. SEMSCH

NEW YORK · 1908

THE TROW PRESS

NEW YORK

TABLE OF CONTENTS

VIEW OF NEW YORK FROM THE NORTH RIVER, 1679
From an old print

This is the first actual view of New York from the North River. It was made in 1679, and the original drawing is in the possession of the Long Island Historical Society. The wagon at the left is going down the original Maiden Lane. The house and lot on the corner, belonging to John Haberding, was sold in 1722 for $600.

Upon the rural acres shown above the commercial interests of ninety millions of people are now centered. To accommodate these interests the ground is covered with steel fireproof buildings of vast area, gained by erecting them from 16 to 47 stories in height. At the point indicated by a cross stands the Singer Building, the highest office building in the world.

Built and owned by THE SINGER MANUFACTURING COMPANY, whose offices occupy all of the Tower above the 31st floor.

VIEW OF NEW YORK FROM THE NORTH RIVER, 1907

ST. PETER'S, ROME, 430 FT.
PHILADELPHIA CITY HALL, 537 FT.
PYRAMID, EGYPT, 489 FT.
CATHEDRAL, SALISBURY, 400 FT.

CATHEDRAL, ROUEN, FRANCE, 490 FT.
PARK ROW BUILDING, N. Y., 382 FT.
WASHINGTON MONUMENT, 555 FT.
ST. ISAAC'S, ST. PETERSBURG, 365 FT.

MADISON SQ. GARDEN, N. Y. C., 305 FT.
ST. STEPHEN'S, VIENNA, 450 FT.

SINGER BUILDING
CATHEDRAL, COLOGNE, 516 FT.

THE SINGER MANUFACTURING COMPANY
ST. SOPHIA, CONSTANTINOPLE, 200 FT.

NO. 149 BROADWAY, COR. LIBERTY STREET, NEW YORK CITY, NEW YORK, U. S. A.

THE GIRALDA, SEVILLE, 350 FT.
612 FT.
CITY INVESTING CO. BLDG., N. Y. C., 489 FT.

THE PANTHEON, ROME, 150 FT.
CAMPANILE, VENICE, 328 FT.

ARCHITECT AND ENGINEERS

ARCHITECT.

ERNEST FLAGG.

DEPARTMENT OF DRAUGHTING.

GEO. M. BARTLETT, *Superintendent.*

Principal Assistants.

CHRISTIAN F. ROSSBORG.
MAX OPPENHEIM.
W. R. C. BIGLER.
A. I. McGLOUGHLIN.
ALBERT PAM.
GEO. W. CONABLE.
W. C. AYRES.
JONATHAN RING.
GEO. A. DELATACHE.

DEPARTMENT OF SPECIFICATIONS.

N. LORENTZ MALMROSS.
J. R. HINCHMAN, *Assistant.*

DEPARTMENT OF ENGINEERING.

O. F. SEMSCH, *Chief Engineer.*

Assistant Engineers.

H. R. HOWLAND.
R. G. RICE.
E. L. H. HUTCHINSON.
C. H. NICHOLS.

DEPARTMENT OF CONSTRUCTION.

FRANK P. WHITING, *General Superintendent.*

Assistant Superintendents.

E. A. ROGERS.
H. J. HOWELL.
C. S. HENEY.
H. P. ORAM.
J. DONOVAN.
O. THOMAS.

CONSULTING ENGINEERS.

FOR STRUCTURAL WORK.

BOLLER & HODGE.

FOR MECHANICAL PLANT.

CHAS. G. ARMSTRONG.
O. E. GOLDSCHMIDT, *Assistant.*

FOR SAFE-DEPOSIT VAULTS.

THE HOLLAR COMPANY.

INSPECTORS.

FOR STRUCTURAL IRON.

ROBT. W. HUNT & CO.

FOR FOUNDATION CAISSONS.

T. KENNARD THOMSON.

INTRODUCTORY

THE many problems encountered and successfully solved in the designing and construction of the Singer Building have attracted such world-wide attention, and so many requests for information concerning the building have been received, that the publication of a history of its conception, progress and completion was decided upon to meet the popular demand for a work of this character.

The material for this book has been furnished by the architect, engineers and contractors who were engaged on the work, and as every detail has been carefully checked and verified, the information given may be relied upon as being correct.

The narrative follows the architect and contractors through each successive step of planning and construction to the time when the new structure was finished and ready for occupancy. Unusual interest has been aroused by the Singer Building, not alone by its height, but because the Tower idea is an entirely new type of office building construction. While the completed building is a monument to the genius of the architect who conceived the plans, and the skill of the artisans who conceived and executed them, yet back of these stands the Singer Company, whose initiative and business acumen made it possible for the architect to put his plans into material form.

THE LOCATION Located in the heart of the financial and wholesale districts of the city, at a point almost equally distant from the upper end of Manhattan and the lower end of Queens Borough, and in close proximity to subway and elevated stations, as well as to many lines of surface cars, the Singer Building is readily accessible from every part of the Greater City.

In the equipment of the building no expense was spared in providing every approved modern device for the comfort, convenience and safety of tenants. The Tower rises high above neighboring buildings, and is set well back from the street line. Thus offices on the thirty-three floors above the fourteen-story basic structure are remarkably free from the noise and dust arising from street traffic.

Tenants of the upper floors have the advantage of a most magnificent view, unimpeded by the walls of adjoining buildings. The Hudson, the East and the North Rivers, constituting the magnificent harbor of New York, flow only a few blocks away, affording an ever-changing panoramic view, while the Jersey Coast, Long Island, Staten Island, Governors Island, the Statue of Liberty, and many other places and objects of interest are distinctly visible.

Tenants of the Singer Building, in addition to the unusual advantages afforded from a business and sanitary standpoint, enjoy the distinction of having offices in a building which has an international reputation and which is the most widely known office structure in the world.

THE SINGER BUILDING
BROADWAY AND LIBERTY STREET, NEW YORK
47 STORIES   612 FEET HIGH

ARCHITECTURAL CONCEPTION

REARING its graceful outlines high above the surrounding buildings, many of which were considered only a few years ago to be marvels of the designer's skill, the Tower of the Singer Building, at the corner of Broadway and Liberty Street, has become as distinctive a feature of the sky line of New York as the Egyptian pyramids are of the Valley of the River Nile.

While the construction of the entire building, from bed rock to flag pole, presented problems that taxed the ingenuity of the architect and engineer, still it is the Tower that realized the dream of the designer, completely revolutionized the prevailing architecture of such buildings, and gave to the Singer Building its world-wide fame.

The architect, Mr. Ernest Flagg, must be thoroughly imbued and governed by the thought that "a thing of beauty is a joy forever," for certainly a more artistic conception than this Tower would be hard to conceive, and it is doubtful if an equally magnificent tower will ever be built unless it is a literal copy of the Singer Building.

In the financial district of Manhattan lying below the City Hall, the available building space is so much restricted and the demand for office room is so great that land values have reached a phenomenally high figure. Consequently, to obtain a fair return on investments there has been a constantly increasing tendency to build in the air what there is not space for on the ground, and while property owners realize that sooner or later some restriction will be placed on the height of buildings, the trouble is to get a restriction that will not destroy the value of land in lower New York.

New York is essentially a "City of Centers," the most prominent of which are the Hotel and Theatrical Section, on Broadway between Fourteenth and Forty-fifth Streets; the Dry Goods Section, on Sixth Avenue between Fourteenth and Thirty-fifth Streets; and the Financial Downtown Section, occupying most of that part of Manhattan Island below Cortlandt Street. The latter section is established by such controlling influences as the United States Customs House and Sub-Treasury; the Stock exchanges; the principal banks, the great insurance corporations; the transatlantic steamship offices, the Produce, Cotton and Metal exchanges.

The business man prefers his office in a location easy of access to these great centers; thus the concentration of great office buildings is found in that part of Manhattan below the City Hall.

Mr. Flagg's solution of this problem is to allow the building to cover the whole area of the lot for a height of say 100 feet, and above that to restrict the area covered by the building to about 25 per cent of the area of the lot—the height being left to economical consideration. In other words, Mr. Flagg would have New York a veritable city of towers, and if the towers were up to his standard of beauty the result would be marvelous.

His contention is, of course, that such construction will allow concentration with the least interference with light and air of one's own and the adjoining property.

It might be recalled here that while our laws have not yet forbidden the erection of a building that cuts off the air and light of the neighboring property, in England they go to the other extreme, so that if one has enjoyed a certain view from his windows for a number of years his neighbors are not allowed to put up any building that will obstruct such view.

GENERAL DESCRIPTION

THE SINGER BUILDING 1897-1906

IN the Spring of 1906 the Singer Buildings consisted of the Singer Building proper, a ten-story structure, located on the northwest corner of Broadway and Liberty Street, with a frontage of 58 feet on Broadway and 110 feet on Liberty Street; and of the Bourne Building, a fourteen-story structure, adjoining the Singer Building on the west, with a frontage of 74 feet 10½ inches on Liberty Street. These two buildings were erected about ten years ago, from plans by Mr. Ernest Flagg.

At various times before 1906 the Singer Company purchased 52 feet, 10¼ inches on Liberty Street, adjoining the Bourne Building on the west, and 74 feet 10¼ inches on Broadway, adjoining the Singer Building on the north.

In the latter part of 1905 the Company commissioned Mr. Flagg to prepare plans for a fourteen-story structure to adjoin the Bourne Building on the

west. This new building was called the "Bourne Building Addition" and will be so designated throughout the description.

About the same time the project of extending the front of the original Singer Building northward on Broadway and erecting a tower of some forty odd stories, 30 feet back of this front, was accepted by the Singer Company, and the plans for this part of the building, henceforth called the "Singer Building Addition," or the "Tower," were begun.

To unite these four buildings into one structure it was necessary to alter the original Singer and Bourne Buildings internally and to carry connecting corridors from the Singer Tower, located on Broadway, at one end of the group, through the old buildings to the Bourne Building Addition at the other end of the group on Liberty Street. Moreover, the old Bourne Building had only three comparatively small elevators. It was decided to change these to four larger elevators, capable of serving not only the old building, but also the Bourne Building Addition. This work was called the "Bourne Building Alteration."

After the scheme had progressed thus far, the Singer Company realized that access to the upper four stories of both the Bourne Building and the Bourne Building Addition, from the corresponding stories in the Singer Tower, would be very difficult because of the gap caused in the group by the lower height of the old Singer Building. The Company therefore caused an examination to be made into the feasibility of increasing the height of the old building by adding four stories.

Accordingly, the architect's engineer, Mr. O. F. Semsch, reported a plan for reënforcing the building through the installation of additional column lines and footings, which was adopted. This work of raising the old Singer Building to a height uniform with that of the Bourne and Bourne Addition was known as the "Singer Building Extension."

It will thus be seen that the improvements really comprised four distinct operations, all carried on at practically the same time, although the work on the Bourne Building Addition was begun first.

A fact worthy of note is that the work was not let to a general contractor, but the various branches were separately contracted for by the owners, under the immediate supervision and direct control of the architect. This arrangement assured greater competition in the taking of estimates, and permitted the

THE TOWER FOUNDATION SEPT. 19, 1906

exercise of greater discretion in the selection of the various subcontractors, than would have been possible under a general contract. It thus resulted in obtaining the best possible workmanship and material throughout. There were more than one hundred different contracts.

The plans for the Bourne Building Addition were filed with the Municipal Bureau of Buildings on April 19, 1906, and approved one month later. After the estimates had been taken, various contracts let and the old buildings demolished, the architect's superintendent took possession of the site on June 16, 1906, began excavating on the 22d, started reënforced concrete foundation on July 16th, and the structural iron work on Aug. 7, 1906.

The plans for the Tower were filed June 29th and passed Sept. 12, 1906.

On Sept. 19, 1906, work was begun by running a steamline from the old building, for operating the air compressor to be used in connection with the sinking of the foundation caissons. On the same day the derricks and hoisting machines were set up and the needling of the adjoining building begun.

On Sept. 24th the excavations were started; on Oct. 1st the material for the first caisson delivered, and on Oct. 25th concreting was begun in the first

caisson, after it had landed at the level, 84 feet, 4 inches below the curb.

The steel work was started on November 20, 1906, by setting the grillage for columns 31 and 32.

The plans for the Singer Extension were filed Dec. 26, 1906, and those for the Bourne Building Alteration, March 27, 1907.

The last foundation caisson for the Tower was landed Feb. 18, 1907, at level 87 feet, 7 inches below the curb.

From that time on the operations proceeded without interruption, there being often over 1,200 men employed daily. The building was practically completed on May 1, 1908, or only one year and eight months after the start.

Compare this with the time it took to erect the Cologne Cathedral, the twin towers of which are surpassed by the Singer Building in height. The Cathedral was begun in 1248 and finished 641 years later—in 1889.

A comparison might also be made with the great pyramid of Cheops, on which 100,000 men were employed for 30 years, which would be equivalent to 3,000,000 men working every day for one year—as against 1,200 men employed every day for one year and eight months on the Singer Building.

[11]

THE BUILDING FOUNDATION

BEFORE beginning construction of the foundations, in order that the engineers might know the exact condition of the soil underneath the site of the building, "test borings" were made by Messrs. Phillips and Worthington in four places, going from 80 to 100 feet below the Broadway curb, not only to the rock but several feet into it. Diamond drills were employed to **TEST BORINGS** remove the cores which were brought to the surface for inspection, which was necessary to prove that the borings had not stopped on a huge boulder deposited by the glacial drift in past ages. These rounded boulders, which abound in the hard pan, are generally of a very much harder stone than the bed rock, which is characterized as New York gneiss or micaceous schist.

Roughly speaking, from the surface to about 70 feet below the Broadway curb the borings indicated what is known as New York quicksand, a material so fine that it will readily flow wherever water will, and while it will safely carry a considerable load, if confined in such a way that it cannot leak out, it is, of course, a very dangerous material to build on where there is any chance of such a leak.

Future cross-town tunnels will undoubtedly undermine many buildings so founded in lower New York. Underneath the quicksand and above the rock was found from 20 to 30 feet of hard pan and boulders, both of glacial deposit.

In some places this hard pan was almost as compact as good concrete and in others it verged into mere sand or sand and boulders. In fact, it was so irregular that not only was the material found in one caisson no criterion for what might be expected in the adjoining caisson, but even what was found in one end of a caisson differed entirely from that in the other end.

Though the original portions of the building are carried on a grillage, or spread footing foundation, 24 feet below the sidewalk, and the first intention was to build the Tower on foundations of a similar character, the engineers, in view of possible subway construction in the vicinity, decided to adopt the pneumatic caisson type of foundation carried to bed rock, which is here about 90 feet below the sidewalk level. Competitive bids were taken and the work was let to *The Foundation Company*, which started work on Aug. 28, 1906, and by working continuously night and day handed over the completed foundation March 1, 1907. In view of the special difficulties encountered this was a very creditable achievement.

The first difficulty which presented itself, and possibly the one requiring the greatest ingenuity to overcome, was the great area **CONSTRUCTION HAMPERED BY LACK OF SPACE** covered by the 30 caissons compared with the total area of the site, which restricted the space remaining for the hoisting frames, tackle, run-ways for the delivery of material and removal of waste, the compressors and other machinery used in the work. As the new part of the building, though of considerable area, has a frontage of

[12]

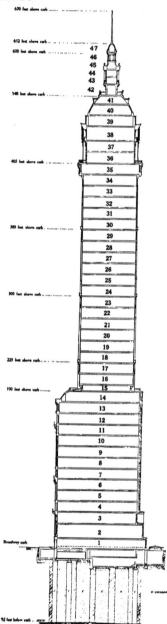

THE TOWER FOUNDATION, OCTOBER 18, 1906

nly 75 feet on one of the busiest thoroughfares in he world, through which all material and excavated oil had to be handled, it will be seen that even the reliminary problems were ones not easy to solve. No sooner were these problems successfully solved han others equally perplexing presented themselves. Concrete had to be prepared, and the machines by which this is done require much space for their operation; the hoisting and delivery into the air locks of the caissons had to be done, and the platforms and raming so designed as to admit this being performed without interfering with other work simultaneously n progress.

In addition to all this, there was the necessity for needling up the walls of the original Singer Building, a heavy and ornate structure, at that time more than 150 feet high. The needling and mats for its support had to be accommodated, still further reducing the available working space.

During the progress of this work a daring and unusual feat in building was successfully performed. It was at first intended to stop the caissons at hard pan, about 20 feet above bed rock, but when it was

decided to go to bed rock, one of the caissons had already been completed 7 feet below the top of

CONTRACTORS EXECUTE DARING PIECE OF WORK

the hard pan, its air lock and shaft removed and the crib filled with concrete.

How to extend this caisson to bed rock was the question which was solved by tunneling through the intervening space from the nearest caisson, excavating the hard pan and underlying stratum beneath the 50 feet of caisson overhanging and filling the cavity below the caisson as well as the tunnel with concrete taken through the tunnel from the adjoining caisson, which, of course, required time and care, for if the entire caisson had been undermined at one time there might have been danger of the great weight of the 50 feet of caisson above breaking loose.

This feat was successfully accomplished by running a small drift tunnel, 5 feet high by 4 feet wide to the farthest end of the caisson above and then excavating vertically downward to bed rock, 15 feet farther, one section at a time and filling each section with concrete from the bed rock up to

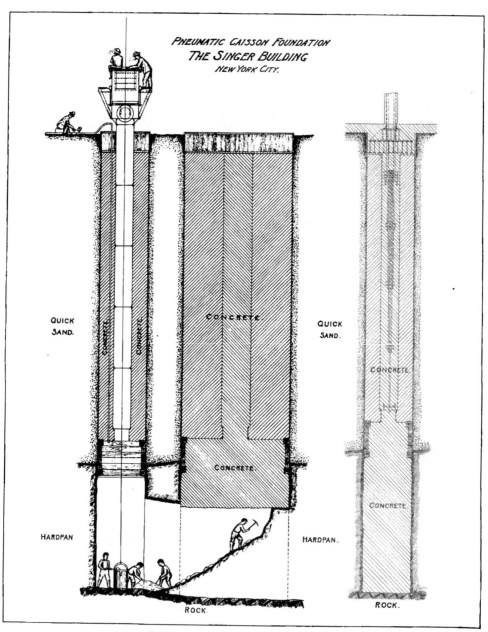

PNEUMATIC CAISSON FOUNDATION
THE SINGER BUILDING
NEW YORK CITY.

QUICK SAND.

QUICK SAND.

CONCRETE

CONCRETE

CONCRETE.

CONCRETE.

CONCRETE.

HARDPAN

HARDPAN.

ROCK.

ROCK.

UNDERMINING ONE OF THE SINGER CAISSONS
(See preceding page)

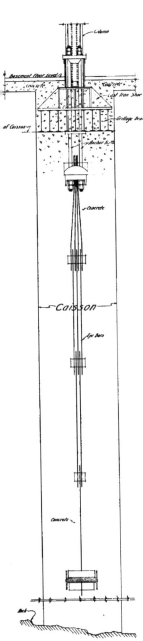

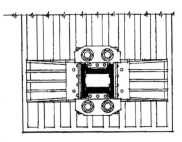

the caisson above before the next section was excavated.

This is probably the first time that a pneumatic caisson has been undermined.

All of the columns are seated on rectangular or circular concrete piers with their footings carried down by wooden pneumatic caissons through quicksand and hard pan to solid rock about 90 feet below the level of the Broadway curb. The piers were built as shafts constructed above the surface of the ground and afterwards sunk to bed rock by men working in the interior chambers.

Ten of the piers were provided with vertical steel anchorages extending nearly to the bottom and built into the concrete. These were made in such a manner as to utilize the full weight of the pier, estimated at 1,150,000 pounds in a maximum case, besides the very large indeterminate friction between the sides of the pier and the earth, which is not counted on, to resist the upward reaction of 925,000 pounds.

The adhesion of the pier concrete to the steel anchor rods, assumed at 50 pounds per square inch, was utilized in designing the anchorages. So securely is the Tower anchored that it would be necessary to exert a force sufficient to pull the caissons out of the ground before the stability of the building would be endangered, and as the cutting edge of the caisson was stopped near the top of the hard pan and the excavation then carried through the hard pan from 20 to 30 feet to rock and the whole space then filled with the best Portland cement concrete, it can be realized that before the caisson could be lifted the concrete would have to be broken in two or else the hard pan would have to come up, too. This would practically mean lifting all the hard pan off of the rock and all the quicksand and water on top of the hard pan—results which could occur only in the wildest imagination.

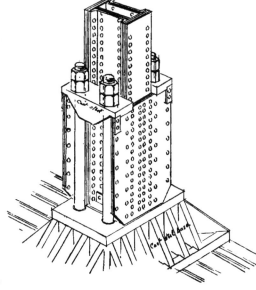

The total weight of the Singer Building, including the Tower, is figured in the vicinity of 165,000,000

[15]

TOWER FOUNDATION, NOVEMBER 20, 1906

pounds and is carried by 54 steel columns. This enormous weight is carried down to rock, at an average depth of about 90 feet below curb, by 30 caissons. These are simply airtight bottomless boxes, square or cylindrical in cross section, having interior chambers large enough for a gang of men to enter and excavate the bottom. The excavated material passes up through steel shafts in the roof. As the caisson extends below the waterline, the compressed air is pumped in to expel the water from the open lower or cutting edge. As the caisson descends there is a greater pressure of air required, which is supplied continuously to the men through an ordinary pipe leading into the working chamber.

This pressure is just sufficient to balance the weight of the water on the outside and thus prevent the water from rushing into the working chamber and taking material from under the adjoining buildings and streets along with it.

As water weighs about 62 pounds per cubic foot,

the pressure at one foot depth is .434 pounds per square inch, or a little less than one-half pound for each foot of depth, or 44 pounds per square inch if the water were 100 feet deep, which is about the limit of human endurance and is in addition to the atmospheric pressure of about 15 pounds per square inch. In the higher pressures the risk of one's losing his life or being paralyzed for life is very great.

The caisson is thus sunk by undermining, by shoveling the material into one-half cubic yard buckets, aided by a heavy weight of concrete, which is added over the roof of the caisson as the latter gradually sinks, and also by additional pig iron blocks, of which as much as 1,200 tons were used on this job. When it has reached a satisfactory hard stratum, which is cleaned and leveled, the whole interior of the caisson and of the shaft connecting the working chamber with the outer air, is filled with rammed concrete, forming a solid monolith upon which the superstructure is readily supported. To permit the passing in

[16]

TOWER FOUNDATION, DECEMBER 5, 1906

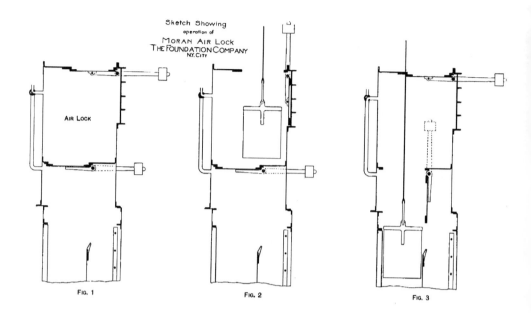

Sketch Showing
operation of
MORAN AIR LOCK
THE FOUNDATION COMPANY
N.Y. CITY

AIR LOCK

FIG. 1   FIG. 2   FIG. 3

and out of a bucket, or of the men from the outside air to the caisson, or vice versa, without excessive loss of compressed air, an air lock or air chamber, invented by Daniel E. Moran, C.E., vice president of The Foundation Company, is used. This air lock surmounts the top of the shaft leading to the working chamber, and by its use it is now possible to sink caissons through quicksand and water, close to adjoining buildings without causing flow of material from under the latter, which, if allowed to occur, would settle and crack them. This is the invention that has made possible the construction of the skyscrapers in Lower Manhattan. The operation of this air lock is described as follows:

When a man desires to enter the working chamber, he first goes into the air lock, closing the outside door tightly behind him. Compressed air is then admitted to the lock until the pressure in it and in the working chamber is equalized. The door between the latter and the air lock then opens by its own weight. The reverse operation of coming out is equally simple. The man climbs up into the air lock from the working chamber, whereupon the lower door is closed tightly. The valve is then opened, which permits the gradual escape of the compressed air from the lock, and when the pressure has been reduced to that of the outside air, the upper or outer door opens and the man steps out. The same description applies to the operation of the bucket, as shown above in Figures 2 and 3.

In the old days of pneumatic caisson work, before the invention of the Moran air lock, the material was carried out in bags of canvas by the men, or was blown out by air pressure through a 4-inch pipe. By means of the recent improvements in this air lock Mr. Moran has made it possible to use a bucket of half a cubic yard capacity almost as freely between the excavation chamber and the outer air as if the work were done in the open.

In fact the bucket has been taken in, filled, brought out, emptied and returned to the air chamber twenty times an hour.

The cement in the foundation was brought to the building in 151,515 bags of 90 pounds each.

QUANTITY OF CEMENT USED If the concrete made with this cement were all loaded on two-horse trucks, it would make a continuous line of 10,180 trucks, 38 miles long, or twice the distance from the Singer Building to Yonkers.

SINGER TOWER—FROM LIBERTY AND WILLIAM STREETS

steel plant, complete rolling mills and a well-equipped bridge shop.

The Singer Building Addition is of the modern type of fireproof steel frame construction. The main part of the building extends up to the 14th

DESCRIPTION OF BUILDING tier; above this point the Tower, 65 feet square, extends up in an almost unbroken line to the 40th tier; from this height springs a segmental dome curving inwardly to the 43d tier, where it is finished with a flat deck; from the deck of the dome the Tower narrows to 12 feet square, its columns continuing up to the 46th tier; from the 46th tier a lantern, 9 feet in diameter at the base, extends above the 48th tier, making a total height from the curb of 612 feet.

On the front of the building there is a two-story curved mansard roof, beginning at the 14th tier and curving inwardly to the Tower at the 17th tier.

At the 36th and 37th tiers the floor extends outside the Tower 8½ feet on each side and is curved to a radius of 37 feet, struck from the center of the Tower; the overhang is supported by cantilever beams extending back into the Tower.

In the basement there are 54 columns; the heaviest carry a maximum combined load of about 1,600 tons, with an area of cross section of about 188 square inches and weighing approximately 800 pounds per

SETTING AN OUTSIDE TOWER BEAM

I N September, 1906, the contract for furnishing and erecting the structural steel was awarded to *Milliken Brothers, Inc.*, office at No. 11 Broadway.

Competition for the contract was very keen, as all of the large structural steel companies coveted the honor of furnishing and erecting the steel work for the greatest skyscraper in the world.

It was found after careful comparison that *Milliken Brothers, Inc.*, were better fitted to handle this great engineering proposition than any of their competitors, because of the convenient location of their immense works at Milliken, Staten Island, N. Y., on tidewater. These works comprise a large modern

BEGINNING OF TOWER STEEL ERECTION, MARCH 16, 1907

lineal foot with connections, etc. Generally the columns are in two-story lengths, although a few of the basement columns are in four-story lengths.

The corner columns, at the southeast front of the building above the fourth story, are carried on a double web riveted girder 30 inches deep and 18 feet long, carrying a load of about 250 tons.

Beginning at the basement, 36 of the columns spaced 12 feet from centers compose the Tower, the four center Tower columns extend up to the 46th tier, while the other Tower columns extend up to the 40th tier from which the dome springs.

There is a total of 850 columns in the building, the heaviest weighing about 28 tons. Above the foundations and exclusive of the columns 17,000 members were required for the floors, bracing and other parts of the building, which will give some idea of the vast number of drawings which were required for this building.

ADJUSTING A COLUMN SPLICE 500 FEET ABOVE STREET

[21]

A special feature of the Tower is the system of bracing employed to provide for the wind stresses.

WIND BRACING OF TOWER The bracing starts at the 39th tier and extends to the foot of the columns, and is composed of heavy diagonal X-braces connected to gussets on the columns at the floor levels and is designed to withstand a horizontal wind pressure of 30 pounds per square foot of surface of the entire vertical surface at the building. The uplift due to the wind stresses is provided for by anchoring six columns of the elevator shaft and four others, or ten in all, of the tower columns by means of heavy pin-connected anchorage bars which extend down about 44 feet into the concrete piers and are built in concrete. The bars are connected with the foot of the columns by 3½-inch and 4½-inch diameter rods which connect with the anchorage bars by means of a heavy cast steel saddle illustrated on page 23. These columns have a maximum calculated static load of 950,000 pounds and a maximum uplift of 540,000 pounds each, due to wind pressure, which is provided for by a cross sectional area of 169 square inches of metal in the basement, the section, of course, decreasing to the top.

This wind bracing is further illustrated and described as follows, as taken from *The Engineering Record* of May 18, 1907:

"The stresses developed by an assumed wind pressure of 30 pounds per square foot on the entire vertical surface of the Tower are resisted by a system of 25 panels of X-bracing between pairs of columns; four of these panels terminate at the 14th floor. Sixteen panels in corners of Tower are continued to the 32d, and the remainder are carried to the 36th floor, just below the dome which surmounts the Tower.

BOLTING WIND BRACING OF TOWER

AWAITING DERRICK LOAD

The arrangement of the Tower bracing is special in order to provide clearance for the doors and windows, which are located between or adjacent to the diagonals. To this end one pair of X-braces forms a panel of comparatively short height vertically at every alternate floor line.

"The spaces between these panels are filled with X-braces forming long vertical panels and providing wide spaces between the diagonals at the upper and lower ends, thus leaving space for a door or window between them, above and below the floor line, which is intersected near the center of the panel. Alternate stories thus have their doors and windows located first in the upper and then in the lower space between the diagonals. In the panels arranged for window openings the horizontal struts at the ends of the X-braces are located approximately symmetrical on both sides of the floor line; in the door panels, the horizontal struts are both depressed just below the floor line so as to leave an unobstructed clearance for the doorway reaching down to the floor level. No knee-braces are used in the bracing system, all diagonal members being full length and provided at their extremities with special horizontal struts, thus forming with the columns complete vertical trusses extending for the full height of the columns.

"In the 32d, or highest regular story, the horizontal struts of the wind-brace system at windows and doors are made with pairs of 10-in. 15-lb. channels, back to back, and the X-braces are made with single 4 x 3-in. x 8½-lb. angles for the long panels, and with 3 x 3½-in. x 6.6-lb. angles for the short panels. In the 30th story the long diagonals change to 7-in. 12½-lb. channels and in the 28th story to 8-in. 13¾-lb. channels, in the 24th story to 10-in. 20-lb. channels, in the 20th story to 10-in. 25-lb. channels, and in the

FIRST TIER, STEEL ERECTION. APRIL 5, 1907

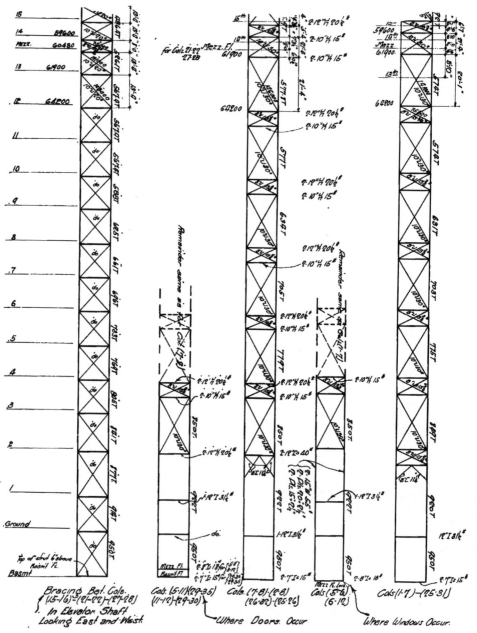

PLAN OF WIND BRACING IN TOWER

BASE OF TOWER, SHOWING WIND BRACING AT CORNERS, AUGUST 15, 1907

SETTING BALCONY BEAMS AND COLUMNS AT 33d FLOOR

14th story 10-in. 30-lb. channels, which are maintained to the basement story. The short diagonals change at the 23d floor to 4 x 3 x 8½-lb. angles, and at the 19th floor to 7-in. 5¼-lb. single channels, at the 12th floor to 8-in. 12¾-lb. channels, which continue the same size through the remaining stories to the basement.

"In eight panels the wind braces terminate at the 2d floor and in eight panels they are carried entirely independent, but at the Broadway front the irregular location of the piers led to a special arrangement and to double grillage beams, as indicated in the part plan. In nine sets of bracing below the 12th floor all panels have full-length diagonals without special provision for window or door openings. In these panels the horizontal struts are all pairs of 15-in. 33-lb. channels and the diagonals are single 10-in. 30-lb. channels. In five panels the bracing terminates at the basement floor where the columns are seated on the grillages and transmit the wind stresses directly to the foundation. In three panels the bracing is extended one story lower to reach the lower end of the columns at the pump-room floor.

"The regular bracing corresponds to the 1st story and all members are shipped separately and field-riveted together at the intersections of diagonals and at extremities to the connection plates shop-riveted to the column. As the webs of the diagonal channels are in the same vertical plane, one of them is cut to clear the other and is spliced across it by a web plate shop-riveted to both pieces and field-riveted to the intersecting channel. The portal bracing between columns in the 2d floor is of two types, one having simple knee-braces connected to vertical web plates riveted between the channels forming a horizontal strut and projecting below their lower flanges, and the other type having semidiagonals attached to the lower flanges of the horizontal struts and braced at their center points with horizontal and diagonal members."

WELCOME TO THE CUNARD S.S. "LUSITANIA," SEPTEMBER 13, 1907

DERRICKS

MAKING FAST A DERRICK GUY

TWO boom derricks were used for setting the steel, one of 40 tons' capacity, which was a special construction designed with a 75-foot mast and 65-foot boom. The mast and boom were made of round timber with cast steel and forged steel fittings. The mast was guyed with eight 1¼-inch steel guy ropes; it weighed about 10 tons and was equipped with ⅞-inch diameter wire rope tackles for the topping and hoisting lifts, which were rove with from 9 to 3 parts, diminishing as the work advanced and the loads decreased. It required about three hours to raise this derrick up two floors as the work progressed.

The hoisting tackle for the 25-ton derrick was rove with ⅞-inch steel wire rope about 2,500 feet long and the lower block had a cast iron counterweight weighing about 1,500 pounds to assist in overhauling. It required about two hours to raise this derrick up two floors as the work progressed.

Chain slings were used for handling all material.

It was necessary to erect a temporary platform of steel and wood on the 14th tier at the front of the building. On this platform the 40-ton derrick was set and was operated with a hoisting engine permanently set on the ground floor. The 25-ton derrick was used for setting the steel work for the Tower; this derrick was operated with an engine set on the 17th floor which was provided with steam from the boiler that supplied the air compressors.

SYSTEM OF OPERATION

The material was hoisted from the trucks by the 40-ton derrick, landed on the platform, then hoisted by the 25-ton derrick and set in place on the Tower.

After setting two tiers of columns and beams the derricks were raised to the top floor and the operation was repeated each time after setting two tiers.

The 40-ton derrick hoisted material from the street to the platform in about one minute and a half, a distance of about 200 feet. Material was hoisted from the platform, about 350 feet, in three minutes.

[28]

SHOWING RECONSTRUCTION OF OLD SINGER BUILDING TO CORRESPOND WITH NEW PORTION

Immediately on receipt of the architect's plans and specifications, a time-table was made up giving

TIME SYSTEM OF WORK the dates for the completion of the various stages of the work. This time-table covered all stages of the work from the making of the drawings to the final completion of the steel work.

A large force of skilled engineers and draughtsmen were employed for several months making the working and detail drawings; a large part of the work was very complicated and the detail drawings had to be executed with unusual care and engineering skill. The accuracy of the drawings and the shop work was evidenced by the fact that when the work was erected the various parts went together perfectly, thereby saving a great deal of time and expense in the field, which is a very important matter.

The first shipment of material from the shops was made Oct., 1906, for the column anchorages, then the material was delivered for the grillages supporting the columns on the concrete piers, after which the heavy cast steel bases were delivered.

Unusually careful preparations were made for the erection of the framework for this great building.

SPECIAL TOOLS AND APPLIANCES Every tool and appliance necessary for the setting of the work was specially selected; the men chosen to take charge of the work engaged the most competent and skilled housesmiths to be had, and every precaution was taken at the very start so as to carry on the work of erection in a faultless manner.

DELIVERY OF MATERIAL Shipments were made from the works on lighters, two complete tiers being shipped at a time, and the erection proceeded at the rate of one tier every two days.

SIGNALING TO HOISTING ENGINE

TIGHTENING A DERRICK GUY

At the 40th tier the heavy steel ribs of the dome had to be erected. The setting of these ribs, which were in two sections, required extreme care on account of the weight of the sections, the great height at which the men were working and the complicated nature of the construction.

Great care was necessary to keep the steel work plumb as the work progressed. The plumbing was done with plumb bobs to exact lines, located on each floor. Wire-rope guys with turn-buckles were used to pull the columns plumb; these guys were left in place until the connections were all riveted. After the erection of the framework was entirely completed the greatest variation in plumbing was found to be $\frac{3}{8}$ of an inch. This was in a height of 575 feet.

AIR REAMING OF FIELD HOLES The field holes connecting the Tower bracing were punched $1\frac{3}{16}$-inch diameter and reamed to $1\frac{5}{16}$-inch diameter in the field; the reaming was done with air reamers.

About 237,000 field rivets were driven with 12 pneumatic hammers, the air being supplied by 2 compressors set on the ground floor, and piped up to the hammers as the work progressed. As many as 1,300 rivets were driven by one gang in a single day, which is a record for this class of work. The rivets were heated in oil furnaces supplied with pneumatic blast from the air compressors.

Approximately 7,000 tons of steel work were used in the Milliken contract for their part of the construction of the building. A temporary electric passenger elevator was installed by mutual arrangement of the contractors engaged on the work to take the men up and down as the work advanced. By this arrangement time and labor were saved and the use of stairs and ladders obviated in going up and down in the building.

THE SINGER TOWER—STEEL STRUCTURE COMPLETE

During the erection of the work hundreds of spectators daily lined the streets and from every

PUBLIC INTEREST IN THE WORK
vantage point breathlessly watched the hoisting of the material from the trucks until it was safely set in place hundreds of feet above the street, while traffic of all kinds passed underneath without interruption.

. The erectors, beginning on the ground floor and gradually working upward to an ever-increasing altitude, until they reached the top of the building—612 feet above the sidewalk—scarcely noticed the change and felt just as secure at the top as they did when they began work on the ground floor.

A notable feature of this work was, that beginning with the raw materials which were made into

LOCAL MANUFACTURE ENTIRELY
steel in open-hearth furnaces, cast into ingots and rolled into plates and shapes in the rolling mills, then transferred to the bridge shops and there sheared, punched, assembled, riveted and machined to proper dimensions, and finally were put into place in the highest building in the world, all the work was done in New York City by New York workmen.

Not a single important piece of material was dropped during the erection and there was not a single fatal accident. This is unprecedented in the history of steel construction and stands as a record for careful and skillful management.

The steel used in the construction of the Singer Building, if made into a ¾-inch wire cable, would

STRUCTURAL STEEL ,
reach from New York to Buenos Ayres, South America, about 7,100 miles. The total length of the steel-bearing columns in the Singer Building is about 53,220 feet, or 10 miles.

The old Singer Building was 10 stories high, and in order to increase the height of the building to the

ALTERATION OF THE ORIGINAL SINGER BUILDING
level of the Singer Tower Building it was necessary to run two new columns near the front of the building, up from the basement. These columns rest on riveted grillage girders and extend up to the 11th tier. The top of these columns supports a cantilever riveted plate girder, which, in turn, supports three columns extending up to the roof.

In the rear of the building, three new columns resting on riveted grillage girders extend up from the basement, and were specially designed to reënforce old columns in the building.

The new columns were made in two lengths for each story so as to facilitate the erection. Holes were cut in the floors, through which the columns passed; as soon as a column was set in position under the existing floor beams, the beams were shimmed up with plates resting on the top of the columns, a section of the beams was then sawed through and removed so as to allow room for setting the next story column, which passed through between the ends of the beams and connected to the column below; this operation was repeated until the new columns were brought up to the level of the 10th tier of the old building. All of this work had to be done at night so as not to disturb the tenants.

Six new floors were put in above the 10th tier; the curved mansard roof was continued along from the Tower building. The curved mansard on this building was very complicated on account of the building being somewhat skewed.

All the new work had to match the connections in the old building. Unusual time and care were used in the preparation of the shop drawings, the result being highly successful, the new work connecting up with the old work without a hitch.

The erection of this work called for a great deal of care and precision, and the erection was carried on and completed in a very quick and satisfactory manner, despite the unusual character of the work.

The steel work for the old building was furnished and erected by the same contractors about ten years ago.

In the Bourne Building, which adjoins the rear of the Singer Building, three old elevators had to

ALTERATION OF BOURNE BUILDING
be removed and four new elevators installed. In order to accomplish this change, it was necessary to put in entirely new framing, requiring much additional framing in the floors around the elevator shafts. In the roof of this building new pent houses had to be built over the elevator shafts; only one shaft could be changed at a time and the work had to be carried on without interfering with the elevator service. This work required a great deal of cutting and fitting in the field to alter the old steel work.

In May, 1907, *Milliken Brothers, Inc.*, were awarded the contract for the ornamental iron work for the Tower Building, and in Oct., 1907, the contract for the ornamental iron work on the old Singer Building was also awarded them. A brief description follows and will prove of interest.

[32]

ORNAMENTAL IRON WORK

THE ornamental iron work was made and erected by the *Whale Creek Iron Works*, as subcontractors under *Milliken Brothers, Inc.* This ornamental iron work alone constituted a very large contract, as architectural iron, both wrought and cast, entered largely into the architect's scheme of ornamentation for the building.

The high Tower of the building owes the light and open effect of the great window bays largely to the use of light architectural iron work, which was employed throughout these bays to form the framework of the windows and consists of cast iron cornices and facias with wrought iron mullions and jambs.

At every 7th story on each of the four façades iron

IRON BALCONIES balconies were erected, supported on ornamental wrought iron brackets. Tons of wrought and cast iron were used in this feature of the building, the setting of which at such a height involved some very interesting problems for the contractors.

All of the stairs throughout the building were made

STAIR RUNS AND RISERS of cast and wrought iron of ornamental design. As it was desired to reproduce the railing design used on the stairs in the older portion of the building, this design was skillfully combined with the string and newel details of a newer type of design, producing a happy result. One of these stairs has an unbroken ascent of 23 stories, and the handrail is made of drawn bronze, fitted into cast bronze newel heads at start and landing of each flight of stairs.

The ornamental cast iron window work entering into the lower 13 stories of the building on the

Broadway and Liberty Street fronts constitutes excellent examples of the iron founder's art, the slender round window mullions with spiral

WINDOW ORNAMENTS fluting and the clearly defined, molded facias, cornices and pediments with leaf and other ornamentation, standing out in strong relief with the bold masonry details, and enhancing the beauty of the principal façades.

Ornamental railings, of wrought iron scroll design, also grace the fronts of the building at certain stories, that at the 11th story being of a particularly heavy and striking design.

The elevator fronts are all of a very fitting design with their combination of wrought and cast iron, and indicate that much study has been given both to design and workmanship. Most of the elevator fronts had to be erected at night owing to the fact that the elevator cars in the older part of the building were in use during the day.

The building has been fitly topped off with a steel tubular

FLAG POLE flag pole extending 62 feet above the collar of the lantern, which is 612 feet above the Broadway sidewalk.

Owing to the fact that the flag pole is set in such an exposed location and forms a very dangerous attraction for lightning, a wooden pole appeared impracticable and the steel construction was therefore adopted.

The pole is mounted on a steel socket set in the lowermost floor of the lantern, and extends upward through the top three stories, a distance of about 30 feet. Inside of the building the pole measures $10\frac{3}{4}$ inches in diameter and it tapers from the collar down to $5\frac{1}{2}$ inches at the tip. The joints were shrunk and caulked and were tested so as to be sure that

[33]

the pole was absolutely air tight before erecting. About 28 feet above the crown collar, the pole has been fitted with two 8-inch sheaves and hoods for a 32-inch time ball, the hoisting cables for which are placed inside of the pole and brought out into an electrical operating winch on one of the lantern floors. The pole is trimmed with a cast steel king pin and two nickel ball bearings, upon which revolves the body of the truck containing two $4\frac{1}{2}$-inch bronze sheaves for the halyards.

The task of mounting this pole on the building was a hazardous one, owing to the extreme length of the one-piece section above the roof, which had to be handled under very trying circumstances before being lowered into the Tower elevator shaft, prior to hoisting it through the ground collar.

After the pole was erected in place it was surmounted by a 12-inch gilt copper ball, the setting of which made a very interesting sight for the crowds of people passing up and down Broadway.

The entire ornamental iron work in the building was completed with notable expedition, despite the fact that unusual difficulties had to be surmounted, not only owing to the great height of the work, but also to the confined floor space and the number of contractors at work within that space.

[34]

MASONRY

FIREPROOFING

IT was the intention of the owners and architect in the construction of the Singer Building to use the most approved means of fireproof construction. To this end, every inch of the steel construction is protected with an adequate covering of terra cotta hollow tile, the standard fireproofing material. It is also used for forming the floors of the building by laying it in the spans between the steel floor beams.

This material was all furnished by the *National Fireproofing Company*, the largest producers of terra cotta hollow tile in the world, and is all of standard approved quality.

Terra cotta hollow tile is a clay product. In the manufacture of hollow fireproofing blocks the clay is burnt to a temperature of approximately 2,800 degrees, so that when fire occurs in a structure fireproofed with this material little damage can result to the material until this degree of heat has been approximated and continued for a considerable length of time.

Terra cotta hollow tile were also used throughout the building for partitions and for furring the exterior walls. The roof construction also is of porous terra cotta hollow tile furnished by the *National Fireproofing Company*, so that the floors, partitions, the coverings of steel columns and girders and the roof are all composed of this fireproof material.

As giving an idea of the great size of this building, it may be said that the *National Fireproofing Company* furnished more than 733,000 square feet of terra cotta hollow tile fireproofing for the purposes described, equivalent in area to more than 16 acres and in weight to 7,800 tons, equal to more than 500 average carloads.

With a building so thoroughly fireproof in its structure, its steel entirely protected, its floors, roof and partitions of this indestructible material, and with all wood and other combustible finish reduced to the barest minimum, any damage to this building by fire, either from fire generated within itself or from fire to which it may be exposed by the burning of neighboring properties, is reduced to a contingency so remote as to be a minor consideration.

FACE BRICK

THE face brick are dark red in color, laid up in English bond, using half brick in the alternate header courses and breaking joint in the stretcher courses; nine courses to two feet. The joints are wide and are raked out to a depth of about half an inch, giving a very beautiful and interesting example of face brick work. This method was first employed in erecting the original Singer Building, about a decade ago, and has since been extensively copied.

One of the bricks at the top of the Tower was made of silver, instead of clay, to emphasize the fact that it is the highest brick in the world. There are, in the entire group of buildings, 5,033,800 brick, of which about 1,000,000 are in the Tower proper. If these brick were laid end to end they would extend a sufficient distance to reach from New York to Detroit, Mich., 635 miles. They would pave a footpath 12 inches wide from New York to Boston, Mass.

The face brick were furnished by the *John B. Rose Co.* of 640 West Fifty-second Street, New York.

BLUESTONE

ABOUT 1,500 cubic feet of North River bluestone were used in the Singer Building construction, comprising templates, bondstones, base courses, window-sills, lintel roof coping and entrance steps.

In addition to the foregoing the sidewalk flagging and street curb entered into this contract, the latter being notable as the largest bluestone curb, "in section," fronting any building in New York City.

All of the bluestone was furnished and placed in position by *Martin P. Lodge* of New York City.

BRICK MASONRY

THIS was one of the largest and most important of all the contracts for the erection of the building. It comprised principally the construction of foundation walls; all the common, face and enamel brick masonry throughout; the setting of all exterior terra cotta; all terra cotta floor and roof arches; terra cotta block furring for walls, columns and partitions; in short, all filling in and encasing of the structural steel framework and all anchors for masonry work.

The brick work was laid up in Atlas Portland cement mortar.

The Tower walls are 12 inches thick at the top and practically 40 inches at the base. From the 14th to the 32d floor they are built with a continuous batter on the outside face amounting to $\frac{1}{8}$ of an inch per story. On account of this novel arrangement the floor space inside the Tower is no less in the lower stories than it is near the top, while the shaft of the building has a slightly tapering effect, adding to its appearance of solidity and stability.

The floors and flat roofs throughout were built of flat terra cotta arches, generally 10 inches in depth, "end construction" type. As the floor beams in the Tower were spaced 4 feet on centers this resulted in very strong floors, capable of transmitting the lateral wind pressure, and adding greatly to the stiffness and rigidity of the building, which, considering its height, are remarkable.

There were 540,000 terra cotta floor blocks used, sufficient to cover an area of eight and one third acres.

Most of the partitions were built of 8-inch by 12-inch porous terra cotta blocks, 2, 3 and 4 inches thick. The steel columns were furred with similar blocks 2 inches thick. All outside walls were similarly furred. There were about 875,000 of these blocks used.

The entire masonry contract was executed by *John T. Brady & Co.* of New York, with Mr. J. P. Butler and Mr. John Dordan of that Company in charge of the work.

THE SINGER TOWER, OCTOBER 20, 1907

MASONRY: CUT STONE WORK

In the building of the Singer Tower 4,280,000 pounds of limestone were used, the greater part above the 33d floor. Handling this stone work was a very difficult operation, because all had to be hoisted from the street side and carried through to position on the other faces. This may seem a simple thing to do, but owing to the intricacy of the structure, crowded with workmen of many trades, it was very difficult.

Nevertheless, the whole operation, including hoisting and setting of stones up to 5 tons in weight, at heights varying from 210 to 520 feet from the street level, was accomplished by the contractors without any accident whatever, a remarkable achievement, in view of the risks attendant on this kind of work.

A very interesting feature occurs above the 33d floor where, supported on tromp arches having a curved face projecting 5 feet, 8 inches, a whole story, crowned by spacious balconies, is carried, the projection of the balcony from the pier face below being 8 feet 6 inches. This was an especially difficult piece of work, as it was impossible to install the steel framework to which the tromp arches are attached until after the stone work was set, and owing to their peculiar form, specially designed centering and falsework had to be used. There are 27 stones, weighing altogether 60 tons, in each of these arches. In hoisting the stone work, which was raised in a single lift from Broadway, 1,900 feet of ¾-inch cable had to be wound on the drum of the hoisting machine, the greatest length by far that has ever been used in a similar operation.

The limestone was furnished and erected by *J. J. Spurr & Sons* of Harrison, N. J.

ARCHITECTURAL TERRA COTTA

THERE are three balconies on each of the four lofty bays in the Singer Tower. They are composed of terra cotta furnished by *The New Jersey Terra Cotta Co.*, 108 Fulton Street, New York City, who also furnished the pilasters, extending upward from each balcony, as shown in this illustration.

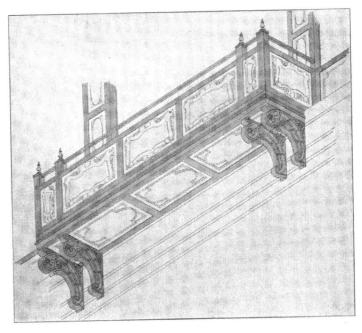

SCAFFOLDING

THE contract for scaffolding was given to the *Chesebro-Whitman Company* of Sixty-fourth Street and First Avenue, New York City. Their work consisted of building the outside scaffolding, temporary elevator shafts and heavy working platforms around the building. This work was particularly difficult and dangerous, but was performed without accident or delay and to the satisfaction of all concerned.

Under a separate contract the *Chesebro-Whitman Company* furnished the first flag pole, rigged with flags, to welcome the steamship *Lusitania* on her first trip to the port of New York. They set the temporary flag pole, 60 feet long, projecting from the west side of the Tower as illustrated. They also supplied the different contractors with their specialties in scaffolding—tool houses, ladders, horses, tubs, wheelbarrows, sand screens, wedges, hose, hods, rope, tool boxes and portable offices.

CARPENTRY

AS the Tower is of fireproof construction throughout, the flooring being of cement and the windows and interior trim of metal, the carpentry contract comprised work principally of a temporary nature, such as scaffoldings and platforms, and some permanent work located mostly in the Bourne Building, Bourne Building Addition, and Singer Building proper. The only carpentry in the Tower consists of show-window work, covered with bronze; oak paneled stools and jambs for these show windows; store doors of oak; some office railings of mahogany and kitchen and pantry dressers of yellow pine and white wood.

A great amount of temporary carpentry work was required for the Singer Building proper on account of the complete removal of the old roof and the taking down of the Broadway and Liberty Street fronts to the 7th-floor level, these portions being rebuilt and the entire structure raised 4 stories in height. Thus platforms were erected in the court about 5 feet wide extending the entire length of the south and east walls, with railings, stairs and hoists; and in the 7th story a temporary weather-proof partition, running around the entire building, about 3 feet back from the front walls, was built, with windows and doors.

The permanent work in the Bourne Addition Building consisted of store and entrance doors and show windows of quartered oak, also of office partitions and some pantry dressers, likewise of oak.

In the Bourne Building it consisted of interior trim and doors, office partitions and railings, all of oak.

In the Singer Building proper, again of interior trim and doors, office partitions and railings, all of oak, from the 7th to the 10th stories; further of show windows covered with bronze, and of the finished and under flooring.

All material for finished work was absolutely clear and free from knots, cracks, sap or other defects, thoroughly seasoned and kiln dried. All interior work, including doors, was hand-smoothed and sandpapered before being set into place; back and edge painted, stopped and primed, face filled or shellaced, before leaving the shops.

Veneering, where required, was not less than $\frac{1}{8}$ inch thick; edge veneering, $\frac{1}{4}$ inch.

New front window sashes in the Singer Building proper, below the 7th floor, were made of clear cherry to match the old work.

All oak was of the best quality quarter sawn American white oak, selected and matched as to quality and color.

The contract included furnishing and setting of "grounds" $\frac{3}{8}$ inch thick, for door and window openings, trim, base, chair rails, picture moldings and wainscoting, in the old building.

Wooden under flooring consisted of $\frac{7}{8}$-in. x 6-in. dressed and jointed spruce, laid close and nailed to sleepers, finished flooring of comb-grained yellow pine with a double thickness of 3-ply rosin-sized building paper between the two.

The Directory Board in the ground floor entrance lobby of the Bourne Building was replaced by one of new design, with ornaments carved according to models.

All of the above carpentry and joinery work was furnished and installed by *C. W. Klapperts' Sons, Suc.*, 328 East Twenty-fifth Street, New York.

EXTERIOR SHEET METAL WORK

THE most striking features of this contract were the ornamentations, hip rolls, crestings and the dormer windows of the dome in the 36th, 37th, 38th and 39th stories; and the turret, technically known as the "lantern," surmounting the dome and forming the crowning feature of the Tower.

With the exception of the floors this lantern consists entirely of highly ornamented copper, built around a steel cage of angle channel and beam work

and the topmost "lift" of the four central columns of the Tower.

Looking at it from Broadway one does not readily realize that the lantern is really 64 feet 5 inches in height, or as high as the average five-story house. It contains the 40th to the 45th stories.

Elevator No. 6, the highest rise elevator in the building, lands at the 40th or Observation Floor. From here steep open stairs and ladders lead to the 45th story, which is the highest "attic" in the world, with the highest "roof scuttle." This is fitted with an ingenious trapdoor, opening outward to form a small platform, more than 600 feet above the sidewalk, from which the Singer flag is raised and lowered.

All of the work consists of 18 oz. cold rolled copper.

Besides the items enumerated above, this contract comprised the furnishing and erecting of all flashings, gutters, exterior leaders, ventilators, skylights, covering or siding of bay windows and roof houses; all roofing, not only that of copper, but also that of slate and tile; and snow guards.

The skylights were made with metal bars and glazed with best $\frac{3}{8}$-inch wired glass, and there are wire guards over them.

To gain light and space, practically all the windows fronting on the interior courts of the Singer Building are built in the form of bays, covered with copper. The siding of the roof houses is of copper clapboards.

The flat portions of the roofs are covered with Akron, Ohio, self-glazed roofing tile, 6 in. x 9 in. x 1 in., bedded in asphalt cement and five layers of heavy tarred roofing felt.

The dome of the Tower is covered with Maine roofing slate, 10 in. x 16 in., $\frac{3}{16}$-in. thick. To get this, likewise the copper work, into place was one of the most difficult and dangerous undertakings encountered in erecting the Tower, as the steeply sloping sides of the dome afforded practically no foothold. The men handling the big sheets of copper at this great height were in constant danger of being blown off and had to be roped on for safety.

This entire contract was executed by the *Herrmann & Grace Co.*, sheet-metal contractors, of Brooklyn, N. Y.

STEEL SASH

THE most prominent feature of the shaft of the Tower, in fact the motif of its design, is the screen of its fifty-seven windows, on the axis of each of its four sides, arranged so as to have the effect of one great window nineteen stories high and 28 feet wide.

Instead of consisting of the customary hollow metal or metal-covered wood construction, these windows, in fact all the windows in the Tower from the 13th Mezzanine story to the top, have solid rolled steel frames and sash, which were manufactured in England by *George Wragge, Ltd.*, and imported by F. G. Draper of New York.

The large curved windows in the dome of the Tower required specially reënforced muntins on account of their great width.

Each of the central windows is about 9 feet high by 10½ feet wide, and comprises fifteen separate sashes, each about 2 x 3 feet.

Nine of these sashes are pivoted top and bottom, opening out for about two-thirds of their width, while the remaining six are stationary. The frames have 5-inch hooks, and the sashes corresponding eyelets, to hold them at the proper distance from the frames, when open.

Both the frames and sash are composed of small "T" bars about 2″ x ¼″ and 1″, with moldings, and L's and ['s about 1″ x 1¼″ x $\frac{3}{16}$″ ingeniously mitred, fitted and screwed together. The movable sash has quaintly shaped grips which add greatly to the interesting appearance of the windows.

On every sixth story of the Tower there are bal-

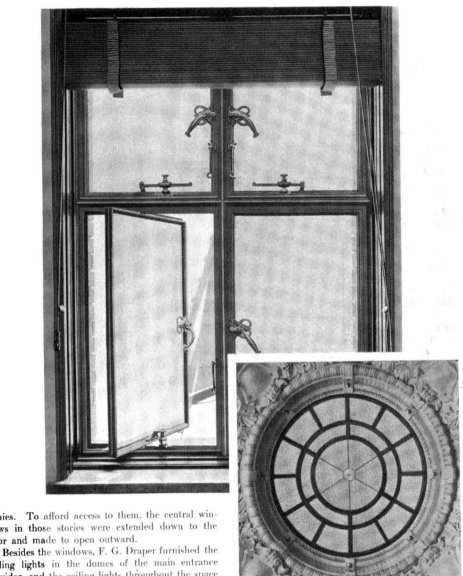

conies. To afford access to them, the central windows in those stories were extended down to the floor and made to open outward.

Besides the windows, F. G. Draper furnished the ceiling lights in the domes of the main entrance corridor, and the ceiling lights throughout the space occupied by The Safe Deposit Company of New York. These ceiling lights are constructed of Wragge bars similar to the windows.

CEMENT AND CONCRETE WORK

PORTLAND CEMENT

ONE of the most important materials used in conjunction with the foundations and masonry work was the Atlas Portland Cement. It was required to conform to the United States Government standard, i. e., it had to be of uniform quality, color and weight, with a specific gravity of not less than 3.10 and contain not more than 3½ per cent. of magnesia, nor less than 60 per cent. of lime. It had to be so fine that not less than 99 per cent. would pass through a 2,500 mesh sieve, and 90 per cent. pass a 10,000 mesh sieve of respectively No. 35 and 40 B.W. gauge wire. The initial set was not to take place in less than one hour, nor the final set in less than three hours.

It had to show a minimum average tensile strength per square inch of 200 pounds when mixed neat; and after setting one day in the air until hard and in water the rest of the time, 500 pounds after seven days and 650 pounds after twenty-eight days. When mixed with three parts of sand it had to show a strength, after seven days, of 165 pounds.

All mortar used for masonry, except for the setting of limestone work, was composed of one part of Atlas Portland Cement to three parts of sand. Concrete consisted of one part of cement, two parts of sand and five of broken stone.

There were about 22,600 barrels of Atlas Portland Cement used in all. At the rate of five barrels to a ton this constitutes 4,520 tons, sufficient to fill 150 cars, or several train loads. It was furnished to the various contractors requiring it at the building in truck-load lots by the *Atlas Portland Cement Co.*, 30 Broad Street, New York.

PLASTERING CEMENT

IN plastering the Singer Building the question of material was given due consideration by owners and architect. Being the entire inside wearing surface, excepting, of course, the floors, it received the most careful attention, and King's Windsor Cement, composed only of high grade materials, compounded with the greatest care, was selected and used exclusively throughout the entire structure.

King's Windsor Cement has stood a time test which the most exacting architects and engineers cannot question. It has been a commercial article for more than twenty years and its merits and superior qualities have been recognized by the best architects, owners and contractors, who have used it for plastering the most expensive Government, State and private buildings, including post offices, college buildings, libraries, public schools, etc.

King's Windsor Cement is sufficiently hard to withstand the roughest usage without marring, yet it is not brittle nor resonant. It is not easily broken and will not transmit sound. The first characteristic renders it invaluable for all classes of work where the plastering is subjected to more than ordinary wear, such as railroad stations. The second characteristic has caused it to be used in the finest residences, hospitals, apartments, dormitories, hotels, etc.

The superior acoustic qualities of Windsor Cement have also been recognized by its being selected for plastering theatres, churches, etc.

This is fast becoming an age of steel and concrete construction and it is absolutely imperative that the plaster, which is applied directly to the metal, should not contain free acid or have any corrosive effect on the metal. King's Windsor Cement fills these requirements. It will not rust or corrode metal, and it is fireproof.

The absence of free acid in its manufacture also warrants expensive decorations in either water or oil colors with satisfaction and perfect safety. King's Windsor Cement will not discolor paper of the most delicate decorations.

The quick drying quality of King's Windsor Cement is also especially valuable. Its easy working qualities are pleasing to the mechanic. It is applied with the same tools and in the same manner as lime and hair mortar, and can be delivered in such quantities as may be required.

This cement is made by *J. B. King & Co.*, office at No. 1 Broadway, New York.

CONCRETE

THE concrete subflooring consists principally in the leveling up of the floor surface in all halls, offices, corridors, etc., to receive the finished flooring, amounting to approximately 300,000 square feet, about 4 inches in depth above the top of the hollow tile arches.

The work was done by *Harrison & Meyer*, No. 16 East Eighteenth Street, New York.

The quantity of material used in this work was about 2,500 cubic yards of cinders, 1,500 cubic yards of sand, and 4,000 barrels of "Atlas" cement.

The floors in all offices were accurately laid within ½ inch of the finished floor level, and those in corridors to within 2 inches of the finished floor.

The upper floors in the Tower, above the 30th floor, have a cement finish over the cinder concrete.

The cinder concrete was mixed in the proportion of 1 cement, 3 sand and 5 cinders.

The materials were mixed in the cellar and raised to various floors by electric hoists, and there spread in place. An average of thirty men were employed in this work, which had to be done principally at night when the building was practically free of other mechanics, in order to save time.

GLAZING

AN unusually large quantity of glass is used in the Singer Building, especially the Tower, which contains, from the 14th story upward, 22,103 square feet; below the 14th story, 15,166 square feet. This is the best lighted office building in New York.

In the old Singer Building, Bourne Building and Bourne Building Addition were used 38,684 square feet, and throughout the entire interior, 9,250 square feet. The total amount equals 85,203 square feet, or practically two acres: enough to glaze a continuous show window, 6 feet high, along one side of Broadway from Liberty Street to Thirty-fourth Street.

First quality American polished cast plate glass was used for all exterior sash in the main fronts, east face of Tower above the 13th Mezzanine, south and west faces above 15th floor and north face above 27th floor.

First quality, flawless, polished wire glass was used for the rest of the window glazing in order to comply with requirements of the Building Department, in lieu of iron shutters.

First quality, 26 oz. acid ground glass, ground on one side only and finished with border and corner rosettes, was generally used for interior sash, doors and transoms.

The glass for ceiling lights in main entrance corridors is rippled, light amber in color.

THE ELEVATOR EQUIPMENT

THE elevator plant was installed by the *Otis Elevator Company*, and is one of the most interesting as well as important adjuncts to the building; interesting because the 40th floor, 548 feet above the sidewalk, is reached by one elevator without change of cars, this being the first elevator ever installed for service at such a height; and important because the measure of the plant's success as an ideal of what an elevator plant should be will, to a very great extent, be the measure of the commercial success of the building.

The three buildings which compose the group are equipped with fifteen Otis Traction Elevators, one short rise Electric Drum Type Elevator and three Direct Lift or Plunger Type sidewalk elevators. These are located and arranged to travel as follows:

In Tower Building: One traction elevator from ground to 40th floor, 548 feet; three traction elevators from ground to 35th floor, 480 feet; two traction elevators from basement to 13th floor, 191 feet; two traction elevators from ground to 13th floor,

176 feet; one drum type elevator from 35th to 38th floor.

Original Singer Building: Two traction elevators from ground to 13th floor, 179 feet; one traction elevator from basement to roof, 204 feet.

Bourne Building: Three traction elevators from ground to 13th floor, 181 feet; one traction elevator from basement to roof, 211 feet.

Each of the passenger elevators, excepting the short rise drum type, has a capacity of 2,500 pounds, at 600 feet per minute speed. The cars have an area of about 35 square feet each, and the highest rise elevator in each group is capable of lifting a maximum load of 5,000 pounds at slow speed. The cars for these elevators are equipped with heavy locking devices for holding them immovable at any landing while safes are being loaded and unloaded.

The machines, which are driven by 40 H.P. 240 volt direct current motors, are located directly over their respective hoistways, thereby giving maximum efficiency and requiring minimum space.

As will be seen from the illustration, the working parts of the Otis Electric Traction Elevator have been reduced to the simplest possible elements. The elevator engine consists essentially of a motor, traction driving sheave and a brake pulley, the latter enclosed with a pair of powerful spring actuated, electrically released brake shoes, all compactly grouped and mounted on a heavy iron bed plate.

Instead of the high speed motor used with the geared electric elevator, a slow speed shunt wound motor designed especially for the service is used.

The armature shaft, which is of high tensile steel of unusually large diameter, is also the driving shaft, and on it are mounted the brake pulley and the traction driving sheave.

The introduction of the direct drive, and consequent elimination of all intermediate gearing between the motor and the driven member, results in a machine of remarkably high efficiency, and the use of the slow speed motor, together with the carefully designed controller, gives starting, accelerating, retarding and stopping effects unexcelled by the far more costly, high grade hydraulic equipments. The stopping, particularly, is accomplished with the greatest ease, and with absolutely no disagreeable effects to the passenger, this resulting from the comparatively low momentum of moving parts following the use of the slow speed motor.

DRIVING CABLES

The driving cables, from one end of which is supported the car, and from the other end the counterweight, pass partly around the traction driving sheave, in lieu of a drum, continuing around an idler leading sheave, thence again around the driving sheave, thereby forming a complete loop around these two sheaves, this arrangement securing the necessary tractive effort for lifting the car. One of the striking advantages resulting from this arrangement of cables and the method of driving them is the decrease in traction which follows the landing on the bottom of the shaft of either the car or the counterweight, and the consequent minimizing of the lifting power of the machine until normal conditions are resumed. Inasmuch as, in any properly constructed elevator, the parts are so arranged that the member (car or counterweight) which is at the bottom of the shaft must come to rest before the other member can possibly come in contact with the overhead work, it will be readily seen that the above mentioned decrease in lifting effort is a very valuable and effective safety feature inherent to this type of elevator.

The cables are arranged with straight leads, thereby increasing their life through the elimination of much of the usual bending and reverse bending, and their durability is further materially increased by the use of ball-bearing shackles or hitches, both on the car and counterweight ends, which are arranged to allow the cables to twist and untwist freely, following their natural strong tendency to do so under the starting and stopping strains, which tendency if restrained results in severe torsional stresses in the cables.

THE CONTROLLING DEVICES

The controller is so designed in connection with the motor that the initial retarding of the car and bringing same to a stop is independent of the brake, the latter being required only to bring the car to final positive stop and to hold it at the landings.

The motor is also so governed, electrically, as to prevent its attaining any excessive speed with the car on the down motion, no matter what the load may be.

In designing the controlling equipment, one of the features demanding greatest consideration, in view of the high speed at which the car runs, was the automatic retarding of its speed and its final positive stopping, automatically, at the upper and lower terminals of travel. This result is very satisfactorily attained with the installation, in the elevator hatchway, of two groups of switches, located respectively at the top and bottom of the shaft, each switch in the series being opened one after another, as the car passes, each operation resulting in a reduction of speed until the opening of the final switch brings the car to a positive stop, applying the brake. This operation is entirely independent of the operator in the car and is effective even though the car operating device be left in the full speed position. The failure of any one of these switches would result merely in the stopping of the car, which could not be run until the switch was put in commission again.

THE SAFETY DEVICES

An elementary feature of security of the greatest interest and importance is provided in the Otis Oil Cushion Buffers. These are placed in the hoistway, one under the car and one under the counterweight, and are arranged to bring either the car or the counterweight to a positive stop, through the telescoping of the buffer—this telescoping occurring at a carefully calculated rate of speed, which is regulated by the escapement of oil from one chamber of the buffer to another. The buffers have been proved capable, by actual test, of bringing a loaded car safely to rest from full speed, and in this respect are unique among elevator safety features of comparatively low cost.

In addition to the safety features already mentioned, the cars are equipped with double-acting wedge-clamp car safeties of Otis construction, which are installed in connection with speed governors, and which are arranged to grip the guide rails securely and bring the car to a safe stop in case, for any reason, the speed of the latter exceeds, by an undue amount, the speed for which the apparatus was installed. The operation of the governor in tripping these safeties also opens an electric switch which cuts off the current supply to the motor, and in case of an emergency the safeties can also be worked by hand by the operator, by means of a lever provided for that purpose in the car. All of the other safety features incidental to a high grade elevator installation, such as potential switches, safety fuses, automatic centering feature in connection with the operating switch in the car, emergency switch, etc., are employed in this installation, and these, together with the simplicity of the installation and the economy of space, resulting from the location of the machine over the hatchway, together with many refinements which have been worked out in the details of the equipment, have resulted in apparatus which gives remarkable demonstrations of the excellence of the type.

All the elevators, with the exception of the sidewalk lifts, will be used for passenger service. The short rise drum type elevator is used for augmenting the service on occasion from the 35th to the 38th floor, being designed for intercommunication between the Singer Company offices, and is of the Standard Otis Worm Gear Electric Type. The hydraulic plunger sidewalk elevators are used for the usual basement freight service, and are operated from a pumping plant and tank system installed especially for this service.

The demands made upon elevator ropes have been constantly increasing until, in the large buildings **WIRE ROPES** of the present day, the ropes used must be practically perfect in material and construction. In the Singer Building, the requirements of strength, speed and, above all, safety, brought forth the desire for a rope as nearly perfect in every way as could be produced.

The ropes were ordered by the Otis Company from the *John A. Roebling's Sons Co.*, the oldest and largest individual wire rope manufacturers in the

world, whose factories are situated at Trenton and Roebling, New Jersey.

Special stock was selected, the wires were specially drawn, and particular care was given to the laying up of the wires and strands into rope.

The result is a series of ropes as nearly perfect in all details as can be manufactured by the most modern methods.

One interesting feature in connection with the elevator installation was the temporary elevator used **TEMPORARY** for carrying the workmen and the **ELEVATOR** less bulky materials. When the steel work had reached a sufficient height a traction machine was installed, with a car running to the 10th floor. Later, the machine, which was located over the shaft, was raised so that the car ran successively to the 16th, 21st, 29th, 32d and 39th floors. These changes were each made in minimum time, usually over Sunday, so that there was practically no interruption of elevator service to the highest point in the building which it was practicable to reach. The use of a high speed elevator for temporary service in a building in course of erection was a novelty, but it worked out very successfully.

Finally, it may be said that the traction type, unique among elevators, is the logical outcome of the tendency of the day toward the greatest possible simplicity, as resulting in maximum economy and the highest degree of safety, and no one can fail to be impressed with the feeling of solidity and substantiality which is, to a remarkable degree, the sensation of the passenger in one of the Singer Building elevators.

ELEVATOR AUXILIARIES AND ELECTRIC TIME RECORDERS

WITH the advent of high buildings requiring a large number of elevators, the question of the best **ELECTRIC** elevator service for handling people **LIGHT SIGNALS** quickly, pleasantly and economically is of the utmost importance.

The earlier forms of elevator service comprised a separate set of buttons for each elevator for signaling to the operators of the respective cars, also a mechanical indicating device on the elevator enclosure which showed the position and the direction of the travel of the car in transit. Such equipments are satisfactory where only one or two cars are involved, with a reasonably short travel to each. Although such mechanical devices are satisfactory under the conditions described, they are a positive annoyance to the waiting passenger when there are a number of elevators in a group, it being obvious that a passenger on any floor must first note the position and the direction of the movement of all the indicator hands upon the elevator enclosure in order to determine which of the elevators is nearest the floor, moving in the direction he wishes to go.

The carrying capacity of the elevators can be largely augmented and the efficiency of operation increased by the installation of the Armstrong Flash Light Signal for signaling to operators and waiting passengers. This system has been installed in the fifteen passenger elevators in the Singer Building.

It is usual to provide at the ground floor a dial for each elevator, these dials having numbers representing the various floors and each provided with a movable pointer, operated by the respective elevator's machinery so as to show the position of said car in the hatch.

Owing to the large number of openings served by the elevators in the Singer Building and the limited space that was at the disposal of the engineer for a dial for each one on the ground floor, it was found impracticable to use a mechanical equipment for this purpose. Instead, an electrical system consisting of rows of miniature lamps, each row representing one elevator with a separate lamp for each opening, was installed at the ground floor for each of the three groups of elevators.

In the Chief Engineer's office was placed another position indicator board showing multiple indications of those given above for all elevators in the building, by means of which the Chief Engineer can, at all times, tell the location of the elevators in any hatch, whether they are performing their proper duty and service, and, if in difficulty, he is able to tell at what point in the hatch the elevators are in distress.

Each group of elevators is equipped with an "up" and "down" push plate on the elevator enclosure at each floor for signaling to the operator. Each car is provided with a signal light, which operates one and a half floors in advance of the floor on which the button has been pushed.

On the elevator enclosures are provided an "up" and "down" light under push button control and set so that the signal will be given to the waiting passenger two and a half or three floors in advance of

INTERIOR OF CAR, SHOWING STARTING AND STOPPING MECHANISM, TELEPHONE AND MEGAPHONE

the arrival of the car at the floor on which the button has been pushed, this service being arranged so that only "up" passengers are served and receive signals on the upward passage of the car, and the "down" passengers when the car is traveling downward.

Each of the elevator cars in the Singer Building is provided with a telephone and megaphone, as shown in the illustration, over the stopping and starting mechanism. This illustration also shows, at the right, two folds of the fourfold door, folded back into the panel. The telephones are connected, through swinging cables and wiring, with a switchboard in the Chief Engineer's office. It has a hinged key board, having a capacity of fifty answering jacks and signals, pro-

TELEPHONE AND MEGAPHONE SERVICE

POSITION INDICATOR BOARD FOR EIGHT ELEVATORS, IN
TOWER BUILDING

are connected into three visual signals in the switchboard, and portable instruments provided with Chapman plugs are furnished with the equipment for the
Chief Engineer's service. This line of jacks being
installed in order to allow mechanics working in the
pipe hatch back of the elevators to have communication with the Chief Engineer's office. With the telephone system is furnished two sets of Helios storage
batteries of ten cells, each having a capacity of 8
ampères.

The megaphones in each car consist of a powerful
transmitter with horn extension. These megaphones
are connected through swinging cables and fixed
wires with the starter's stations in the respective
sections of the building. A special starter's box in
each section is arranged with a series of keys so
that communication can be had by means of the
starter's telephones with either the Chief Engineer's
office and through the switchboard to any station on
that equipment, or by other keys he can communicate
any message or instructions he may desire to any one
or all of the operators in the cars; the megaphone
system being arranged so that the operators cannot
talk back. This equipment forms a very valuable ad-
junct in the equipment of the building, enabling the
Chief Engineer or any of those engaged in the service
to communicate directly with the parties interested.

Power for operating the signal service, the bell service in the building and for charging storage batteries,

ELECTRIC POWER FOR SPECIAL SERVICE is furnished through a bell switchboard placed in the engine room,
power for which is supplied by
four Diehl type "E" No. 4 Motor
Generators, all operating from a
240-volt circuit. Two of these supply power at 75
ampères, 15 volts on secondary circuit and two at 100
ampères, 15 volts.

The switchboard is supplied with Weston volt and
ammeters, with a four-point switch and shunts for
testing purposes for each. The board is also provided with a battery charging rheostat having a capacity of 25 ampères and sufficient resistance to permit
charging a single Helios cell of 8 ampères operating
on a 15-volt generator circuit. Further, with switches
to operate the electroplating system, if desired, also
to operate bells, phonographs or other special services
in the building. All switches are "back-of-board"
type using enclosed fuses. The Shunt Field Regulators and motor starting switch are the Cutler
Hammer "back-of-board" type. The switchboard
is Italian marble, supported on copper pedestals.

vided with five cord circuit, operator's telephone circuit and one night alarm circuit.

Telephones are also located at the special starter's
station boxes in the three sections of the building,
also in the elevator machine rooms on the 13th floor
Mezzanine, 36th floor Mezzanine, 39th floor Mezzanine, 42d floor Mezzanine, pent house, Singer Extension pent house, Bourne Building pent house, Engineer's room, boiler room, repair shop and engine
room; the equipments being the standard central
energy equipment.

In addition to the equipment described, a line
for telephone service is run from the telephone
switchboard in the Engineer's office up through
the Tower to the 41st story, having Chapman floor
boxes at each landing. The wires for this service

Each of the elevator openings throughout the building is provided with a pneumatic door opener and closer of a new and unique design, the special feature of which is a differential action, giving the maximum power at the point of opening, also at the point of closing, and minimum use of air. Its slowest speeds are at the points of opening and closing and the maximum speed of opening or closing is at the halfway point.

AUTOMATIC OPERATION OF ELEVATOR DOORS

Another feature of the device is that it has a positive lock when open or closed, thus giving absolute assurance that the door cannot be opened from the landing without the proper instrument for operating the valve in the hatch. These devices are operated through a cam attached to the top of the elevator, operated by foot treadle in the car. The air which operates this device is furnished by a Clayton Air Compressor, at 30 pounds pressure, located in the engine room. The air before reaching the door opened and closed is passed through a mechanical arrangement whereby a certain amount of lubricant is carried forward, thus insuring the automatic lubrication of the devices at all times.

An especial feature of this equipment is the pneumatic door opener and closer on the ground and first Mezzanine floors, where the doors themselves are solid bronze, four panels, folding type. These doors are very heavy and the device succeeds in opening from a straight line position and closing to a straight line position.

ELECTRIC TIME RECORDER

In the Chief Engineer's office there are five 8-inch Electrical Time Recorders, made by the *Bristol Manufacturing Co.*, and mounted on a white Italian marble board. These instruments are connected to the five generating sets in the power plant for recording their time of operation.

CIRCUIT BREAKER AND EMPLOYEES' INDICATOR

As a supplementary equipment to the position indicator board in the Chief Engineer's office, there are small lamps operated from the various machine rooms showing the Chief Engineer where the employees are located. Each circuit breaker on the electric elevator control in the various machine rooms are connected with miniature lights installed on part of this board so that the Chief Engineer may know which circuit breaker in the group is open.

This installation was made by the *Elevator Repair and Supply Company* of New York.

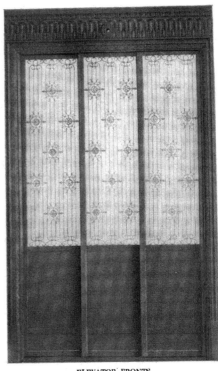

ELEVATOR FRONTS

The elevator fronts for the 2d to 40th floors inclusive, and for the shuttle elevator 36th to 39th floors, were furnished and erected by the *Hecla Iron Works*, manufacturers of architectural bronze and ironwork, North Eleventh and Berry Streets, Brooklyn, N. Y. The doors are twofold, arranged to slide back of a standing leaf, so that when they are closed the front consists of three panels, as shown by the illustration.

Both doors and standing leaves are constructed with wrought iron frames. Each is divided into an upper and a lower panel. The lower panels are filled in with No. 12 B. & S. gauge sheet iron, perfectly flat and smooth, secured into place with moldings.

The wrought iron grillework is ornamented with cast-brass rosettes, spaced at regular intervals, as shown on the illustration. As all the ironwork is finished in dull black, the contrast between it and the brass rosettes is very effective and pleasing.

ORNAMENTAL BRONZE AND MARBLE WORK

interior decoration is again finding due appreciation. In the last decade especially the finest ornamental bronze of domestic manufacture has been used, and lavish use has also been made of fine marble.

Nowhere, however, in recent work has greater advantage been taken of the possibilities of the enrichment of marble by the use of decorative bronze than in the Singer Building. It is in this use as well as for the more strictly utilitarian features, such as doors, railings, etc., that is found the great beauty of the main corridor of this building.

The marble, though beautiful in itself, is greatly improved by combination with the bronze, and it is the effect of this combination that has given this corridor the distinction which places it a step in advance of other fine interiors.

Entrance to the corridor is through a bronze doorway of graceful grille construction. The design consists of bars and scrolls, the transom carrying a clock framed in finely modeled ornamentation. The doorway is 24 feet high by 13 feet wide, and contains more than four tons of bronze. This bronze work and all other ornamental bronze work in the building is from the foundry of *Jno. Williams, Inc.*, New York.

On the marble columns and walls in the main corridor there were used more than 3,600 lineal feet of cast bronze ornamented molding, also eighty medallions, each bearing the trade-mark of The Singer Manufacturing Company.

Other notable features are the bronze fourfold elevator doors and transoms, main stair railings and balcony, railings, doors to the office, two bracket lanterns, one on either side of the main entrance, bronze master-clock on main stairs in lobby and bronze directory frames. Altogether, the firm of *Jno. Williams, Inc.*, has installed in this building more than 75,600 pounds, or nearly 38 tons of ornamental cast bronze. The intrinsic value of this metal is enhanced many times by reason of the expensive nature of the labor of artists and artisans expended upon it in its manufacture. In work of this character, before a pound is cast, costly models must be made. The castings from these are finished by hand chasing and the parts are fitted together with an exactitude not excelled in any other mechanical art, the completed work being of the highest order of workmanship. The color is of the rich natural hue of bronze, no artificial coloring or "patine" being used.

This richness of color is due to the fact that the

T HE beauty of combining bronze and marble was known to the earliest workers in these materials, extensive use being made of them to enrich their temples of worship and the costly palaces of their kings.

Ancient records tell of the lavish use of bronze in these buildings, and the ruins of ancient cities still show traces of this early magnificence in interior decoration.

That the art of bronze working should, so early in the world's history, have attained such a high degree of excellence is not to be wondered at considering that it is one of the earliest of the arts, the age of bronze, in fact, beginning at a time that antedates the record of authentic history, following the age of stone, in which the history of primitive man is veiled in mystery.

It is only in recent years that ornamental bronze has been made in this comparatively new country, but we are now surpassing the ancients in the splendor of the interiors of our buildings as we have already surpassed them in size; and the use of bronze for

WEST END OF MAIN CORRIDOR

alloy used is the United States Government Standard, 90 per cent. of pure copper and 10 per cent. of tin and zinc. This color will mellow slightly with time, but will practically be as everlasting in tone as the colors in the marble; hence, so long as this building stands the rich beauty of this interior will exist in its present form to gladden the eye of the critical beholder.

MARBLE

THE first thing that impresses the visitor upon entering the Singer Building is the artistic charm of the vista which stretches away from the entrance, through the main corridor, to the bronze clock at the rear. This delightful view is bounded its entire length on either side by massive marble piers, and the whole effect is one of regal richness.

But it is only when the details of the decorations are examined that one fully realizes the blended beauties here displayed. A wealth of delicate tints and pleasing colors appeals to the artistic sense with irresistible force, without a discordant note to mar the general harmony.

To the composition of this attractive picture sunny Italy has contributed of her choicest products. Every grand pier in the two rows is faced with Pavonazzo marble—the finest and most beautiful marble in the world—set in a fitting frame of silver-gray Montarenti Sienna, while the corners are trimmed with beaded bronze. The Pavonazzo marble was selected with extreme care and prepared with expert skill. No block was accepted which was of too dark a shade or had stronger markings than would harmonize perfectly with the light color scheme. This necessitated the discarding of many otherwise perfect blocks, but the splendid result amply justifies such strict requirements.

The same material, revealing artistic Nature in her happiest mood, is used in the wall finish and the door and elevator trimmings. The effect obtained in the wall panels and tympanums, in which the pieces are matched with extreme care, being particularly striking.

Surrounding the upper portion of the corridor are bronze-trimmed balconies; at the tops of the grand piers are bronze medallions bearing the Singer monogram, while overhead in the series of domes that compose the ceiling are set circular pieces of rippled glass through which the light from hundreds of electric lights is gently diffused throughout the corridor.

At the rear, stairs of fine Italian veined marble lead up to the bronze clock on the first landing, where the stairway divides into two flights, leading to either side of the building.

The production of the superb effect presented by the main corridor of the Singer Building is a monumental achievement—a tribute both to the sunlit hills of Italy and the artistic efficiency of American craftsmanship.

The marble work throughout the Singer Building was all done by the firm of *Batterson & Eisele*. This firm has unlimited resources for securing the finest quality of material, employs only artisans of the highest skill, and owns a manufacturing plant equipped with the most effective machinery that human ingenuity can devise. Its plant is located at Edgewater, N. J., on the Hudson River, opposite General Grant's Tomb, where it occupies an area equal to 100 city lots. It has executed the marble work on many of the most important buildings throughout the United States.

TILE WORK

THE tile work throughout the building was executed by *Herman Petri*, No. 101 East Seventeenth Street, New York City, and is an important feature of its interior finish.

In the space occupied by The Safe Deposit Company of New York, under the Broadway and Liberty Street sidewalks, the side walls as well as the walls in the passages out of the main entrance, the ladies' rooms and directors' offices, are all tiled in a unique and pleasing manner, an attractive effect having been obtained through paneling the entire work. Colored tiles mark the borders of the panels, the body tiles having a rich cream or ivory noncrazing mat finish. All are the product of the *American Encaustic Tiling Co., Ltd.*

These tiles have also been extensively used in the coupon rooms, where they are subjected to a severe overhead light.

The floors of the basement, engine rooms and passages are covered with a rich red unglazed floor tile; while the barber shop and the toilet rooms throughout the building have floors of alabaster white vitreous ceramic tile, all manufactured by the above-mentioned concern.

The walls of the Engineer's office, the barber shop and the 33d floor dressing rooms are tiled with glazed tile of American manufacture.

CENTER OF MAIN CORRIDOR, LOOKING SOUTH

PLUMBING

TWO WORTHINGTON HORIZONTAL DUPLEX FIRE PUMPS: CAPACITY 1,000 GALLONS PER MINUTE

THE buildings are supplied with water through five street connections—two taken from the Broadway main and three from Liberty Street. Three of these mains (one from Broadway and two from Liberty Street) are combined into one header after passing through Worthington meters and connected and by-passed to water jackets of ammonia coils, having sixteen $1\frac{1}{4}$-inch valved connections on supplies and returns, so arranged that any coil can be shut off for repairs without interrupting the operation of the ice plant.

After passing through these coils (situated in the old Singer Building) the water is run through a tunnel to a 7-inch Croton water header in the Tower, to which the remaining two mains also are connected. From this header the water passes through two specially designed horizontal Scaife filters into an 8-inch header from which the supplies to two suction tanks (combined capacity 10,000 gallons) are taken, controlled by "Ford" float valves.

The outlets from the suction tanks are collected into an 8-inch header and run through a tunnel to the high and low pressure house pumps and fire pumps.

The pumping plant consists of two high pressure, compound, direct acting duplex Worthington steam house pumps; two similar low pressure house pumps and two high pressure fire pumps. The details of these pumps are given in the introduction to the chapter on Mechanical Plant.

These six pumps can all be used for fire purposes combined with the Fire Department steamers. The two low pressure pumps supply water to four house tanks on the 13th Mezzanine floor, of a combined capacity of 6,000 gallons, all cross connected for house supply and fire purposes.

All water used from the 13th floor to the basement, in the four buildings, is supplied from these tanks.

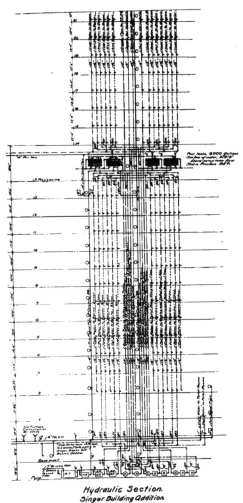

Hydraulic Section.
Singer Building Addition.

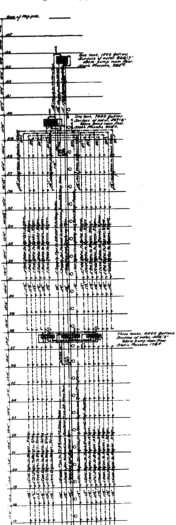

The high pressure pumps feed three house tanks on the 27th floor, of a combined capacity of 5,000 gallons, one on the 39th floor of 7,000 gallons capacity, and one on the 43d floor of 1,500 gallons capacity, through one pump line.

The 27th-floor tanks supply from the 26th story down to and including the fixtures in the 13th Mezzanine story and the roof houses of the Singer Building and Bourne Building.

The tank on the 39th floor supplies from the 35th to the 27th stories inclusive; connections are also taken from this tank to supply the high pressure hot water and ice water systems.

The 43d-floor tank supplies the fixtures from the 39th to the 36th stories inclusive.

Owing to the wind bracing in the steel construction, these nine house tanks had to be set into place directly after the floor framing under them had been erected.

Seven of these tanks were hoisted into position, while two of them, those for the 39th and 43d floors, had to be assembled in place. The 43d-floor tank has a 12-inch sleeve passing through it to accommodate the flag pole, which extends down to this floor.

There are five 6-inch standpipes extending from the basement to the 13th floor and one each from the 14th and 43d floors, with over one hundred 2½-inch fire hose connections in the combined buildings. There are also hose connections on the roofs of the Singer Building and Bourne Building, from which water could be played on the adjoining buildings. Each of these fire outlets has 75 feet of hose, which, together with the valve, rack and nozzle, are placed in specially designed boxes set into the walls flush with the finished trim, thus offering no obstruction in the stairways and corridors, as fire appliances usually do.

There are siamese connections for the Fire Department steamers to attach to—three on the Broadway side and two on Liberty Street.

All office basins throughout the Tower are supplied with cold, hot and ice water. There are two hot water heaters, one for the high pressure system, tested to 500 pounds, and one for the low pressure system, tested to 250 pounds.

The high pressure hot water system is supplied

from the 39th-floor tank through a 4-inch down supply running to the hot water heater. From there a 3-inch hot water riser is run up to the 13th Mezzanine floor, where it branches horizontally on the ceiling and feeds eight risers extending up to the 39th floor, supplying

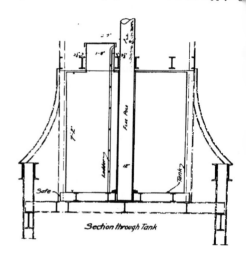

Section through Tank

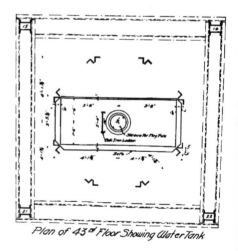

Plan of 43ᵈ Floor Showing Water Tank

lavatories and private toilets. These eight risers are collected into a 3-inch return, which is carried back to the heater in the basement, a drop of about 550 feet, to insure good circulation. Branches are taken off this pipe to supply the public toilets on the 35th to the 14th floors inclusive.

The hot water heaters are supplied with live and exhaust steam, and controlled by Davis and Roesch regulators.

There is a high pressure ice water system for the Tower. It is supplied from the 39th-floor tank, and filtered a second time by being passed through a

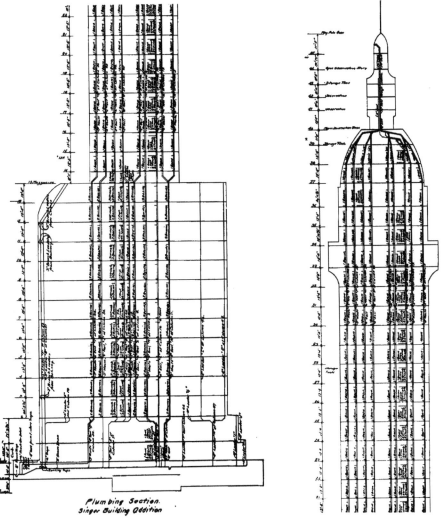

Plumbing Section.
Singer Building Addition

ILLUSTRATION OF PLUMBING FIX-
TURES, SHOWING VARIOUS POSI-
TIONS OF METAL DOORS TO
RECEPTACLES FOR PIPING AND
ACCESSORIES

specially constructed Loomis Manning filter, tested to 500 pounds. Leaving this it flows to the ice water cooling tanks, and thence to the ice water circulating pumps which force it up to the 39th floor through four risers, and return it through four circulating lines back to the cooling tanks. The ice water is thus circulated continuously and its volume replenished from the 39th-story tank. The ice water piping is covered with a cork insulation 1½ inches thick.

All cold and ice water piping subjected to excessive pressure, on account of the great height of the building, is made of extra strong galvanized wrought iron pipe. On the plumbing section drawing are indicated the large soils, wastes and vents which had to be installed, and the method of connecting them together at the top.

The contract included the furnishing and setting of about 750 new plumbing fixtures, with their accessories. The method of concealing all piping about the office basins, and making the valves accessible by means of metal doors placed under the fixtures, as shown in the cut of the fixtures on page 60, is of particular interest.

PLUMBING, BOURNE BUILDING ADDITION

The plumbing work in connection with the Bourne Building Addition is a splendid example of modern up-to-date plumbing. Great care has been taken in the selection of the various materials and fixtures and mode of installing them. All underground piping is of extra heavy cast iron, each area line, leader and floor drain is properly trapped, each trap having cleanout screws of extra heavy cast brass accessibly placed. All leader, soil and vent lines above the basement and grade are of extra strong galvanized iron pipe, and supported by clamp hangers of the most recent pattern. The fresh air for the sewerage system is supplied by a 6-inch "Perfect" fresh air intake, extending to the open air. The floor drains are of bronze, with removable strainers. The area and floor drains are connected to a "sump" pit, which is automatically emptied by a motor-driven submerged pump specially built for the purpose.

The fire protection for the building is most thorough and complete. It consists of 6-inch extra heavy galvanized standpipe, extending from a siamese connection 6 inches in diameter with two 3-inch outlets, Fire Department pattern, to the main house tank system, and has at all times a direct pressure of 300 pounds to the square inch. This standpipe is also cross connected to the fire and house pumps in the basement. On each floor there is an equipment consisting of a hose reel containing 100 feet of 2½-inch best linen hose controlled by a 2½-inch red metal fire valve, with nozzle, etc., complete. This part of the work has the approval of the Fire Department and Board of Fire Underwriters of New York City.

Each stack of fixtures is supplied with hot and cold water and a return circulation. The cold water supplies are of extra strong galvanized iron pipe and the hot water of soft annealed brass pipe. Where the least danger from frost or atmospheric condensation exists the supply pipes are covered in the most approved manner, and are canvased, ringed and painted.

The fixtures are all class "A" and as selected by the architect. There were installed 9 water-closets, 107 basins and 1 shower bath. The words "J. L. Mott Iron Works" stamped on each of these fixtures guarantee them to be of the highest quality and efficiency.

The closets are of the siphon-jet type with "Simplex" valves. The urinals are the "Metropolitan" with "Integral" traps and "Presto" push-button flush valves, the basins principally of the "Claremont" pattern with integral back and "Hygeia" wastes. The slop sinks are of "Imperial" porcelain protected by pail guards. All metal work in connection with these fixtures is of red metal, heavily nickel plated.

Sufficient gas-fitting has been supplied to light the basement toilet rooms and the corridors in the event of failure of the electric plant.

The work has been executed and installed in the most thorough and workmanlike manner, under the personal supervision of the plumbing contractor, *Chas. H. Darmstadt*, No. 352 West Forty-third Street, New York City.

PLUMBING FIXTURES, SINGER ADDITION

ONE of the most important questions to be settled by the architect, owners and engineers in connection with the mechanical equipment of the Singer Addition, was that of plumbing fixtures.

It was felt that a building of so unique and distinctive a type deserved in this, as in other lines, the best that money could buy. After a most careful examination of the fixtures of various manufacturers, it was finally decided that those designed by the *Henry Huber Company* (now *Federal-Huber Company*) should be installed.

These embodied all the elements of style, durability, cleanliness and economy in installation and operation that those interested desired, and working tests have completely proved the wisdom of this choice.

The lavatories vary in type to suit conditions, but are all of the best quality vitreous china, with special center leg and wall supports and are supplied with hot, cold and ice water by means of self-closing, push-button controls. The majority of the lavatories are of the design illustrated herewith and the connections, with the exception of the trap, are all concealed within a specially designed boxed back. This fixture (copyrighted as "The Singer Lavatory") is made complete with a heavy nickel-plated cast brass attached soap dish and, in the offices, plate glass mirrors with nickel-plated brass frame; glass shelves and glass towel bars are added.

The water-closets are of vitreous china, of heavy design, with sanitary rim and base, and are attached to the waste pipes with the Huber Special Sanitary Screw Connection.

Heavy seats of quartered oak, carefully joined and highly polished, are attached to the closet bowls with heavy nickel-plated brass hinges. A thorough and economical flush is obtained by means of the Huber Automatic Slow Closing Flush Valve.

Huber's siphon-jet vitreous china urinals are installed and these are flushed by means of a smaller type of the flush valve used with the water-closets.

Heavy vitreous slop sinks are installed conveniently throughout the building. This fixture was as carefully selected and equipped as those previously mentioned; and with large waterway slop sink faucets, minimizing the time consumed in drawing water; a heavy brass pail guard, to prevent breakage; and a full sweep trap standard that cannot become clogged, it is as complete as its uses require.

The extreme height of this building made the water-pressure problem a most serious one. Water tanks are placed on the 14th, 27th, 39th and 43d floors, and absolutely to insure an equalizing of the pressure at the fixtures all of them are equipped with the Huber Company's Gem Reducing Valve.

In addition to the fixtures mentioned, a number of special bath tubs, needle baths and showers are installed, perfecting the plumbing equipment of this most modern office building.

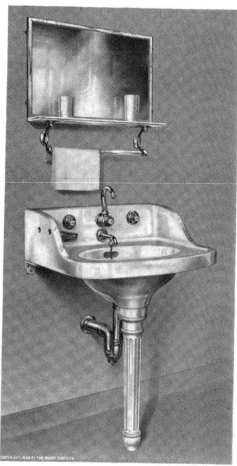

HEATING AND VENTILATING

THE building is heated by a double-pipe overhead-fed vacuum return steam system, with automatic thermostatic temperature regulation. Exhaust steam from the engines is used for the heating, supplemented by live steam supplied through a pressure-reducing valve.

Practically, the entire building is heated by direct, pressed steel radiators. In the important rooms, such as the north banking room in the 1st story, and the principal offices of the Company in the 33d and 34th stories, these radiators are enclosed in ornamental bronze screens.

The main corridor on the ground floor, also the safe deposit vaults in the basement, are heated by an indirect system, the heating surface of which is located in a central stack room in the basement.

The fresh air supply for this indirect system is obtained from the large light court at the rear of the Bourne Building and Bourne Building Addition. The air is drawn through a water air-washing device and a tempering coil by means of direct connected electrical blowers, after which it is forced through the stack chamber and ultimately delivered into the rooms through galvanized iron ducts and ornamental bronze registers. All parts of this system are thermostatically controlled.

The piping system for supplying the radiation throughout the Tower consists of a 12-inch riser, extending from the basement, back of elevator No. 6, to the 39th floor. Here it supplies a horizontal main from which are fed risers ascending to the 45th and descending to the 13th Mezzanine floor; the latter have expansion loops in the 31st and 21st stories.

The return risers, corresponding to the above, fall to the 13th Mezzanine, where they are collected into one 4-inch return riser, extending down to the basement, behind elevator No. 6.

The lower part of the building is supplied by a 10-inch riser extending to the 13th Mezzanine floor, where it branches horizontally and feeds a number of down supply risers. The return risers run parallel to the supplies. Each has one expansion loop. The main risers have expansion slip joints, the 12-inch riser having two. All risers are valved independently.

Most of the radiator connections are run under the floors with galvanized iron covers over them. Practically, all radiators are thermostatically controlled on the supplies and all have vacuum valves on the returns.

All piping is covered with 85 per cent. carbonate of magnesia, canvas jacketed, except radiator connections under floors, which have air-cell coverings.

VENTILATING All toilet rooms are ventilated through registers, into shafts extending upward, from which the air is exhausted by means of directconnected electrical fans, the principal one of which is 70 inches in diameter, located on the 39th floor.

VENTILATION OF MECHANICAL EQUIPMENT The heated air from the engineering department is exhausted by means of a large fan delivering to a court and the fresh air to supply the air exhausted is drawn, by similar fans, from light space in rear of building. At the intake of this duct there is a corrugated iron and glass house, containing a Webster Air Washer and Humidifier, which presents novel features of construction.

The air to be washed, humidified or cooled passes first into the spray chamber where it is thoroughly washed and cleansed by passing through from two to four sheets of water, having a combination "rain-and-spray" effect.

The "rain-and-spray" effects, produced by special patented copper heads, were selected because it was found that sheets of rain more effectually removed dust and dirt from the air, whereas sheets of finely divided spray, on account of the more intimate contact possible between the air and water, had a greater cooling effect.

After leaving the spray chamber the air passes through the eliminator, where all entrained water or unevaporated moisture is entirely removed, thence through to the ventilating system into the building.

The special feature of the Webster Eliminator is the use of horizontal baffle plates, superior to the various vertical types generally used, in that any entrained water deposited upon the baffle plates is carried off at once horizontally to a gutter and returned to the water tank, thus preventing re-contact with the lower strata of air passing through the eliminator.

A water tank or sump contains the spray water, which is circulated at from 2 to 20 pounds hydrostatic pressure by means of a centrifugal pump, electrically operated from the main power plant.

TEMPERATURE REGULATION

ON THE LEFT THE ILLUS-
TRATION SHOWS THE VALVE
GOVERNING STEAM SUPPLY
AND ON THE RIGHT THE AD-
JUSTABLE THERMOSTAT AUTO-
MATICALLY GOVERNING OPER-
ATION OF VALVE TO KEEP THE
TEMPERATURE UNIFORMLY TO
THE POINT DESIRED

IN connection with the heating plant for the Singer Building, a system of automatic heat regulation has been installed throughout.

In every room a thermostat is conveniently located which controls the heat sources in the room by operating the valve on the steam supply of the radiator or radiators. The Johnson System of Automatic Heat Regulation was installed in the old Singer Building and later in the Bourne Building, and the same system has been adopted and installed by the *Johnson Service Co.* of Nos. 36 and 38 East Twentieth Street, New York, throughout the different sections of the completed Singer Building.

By this system the temperature is kept uniform during the season in which artificial heat is required, and the different rooms can be kept at different temperatures to suit the desire and convenience of the occupants.

Compressed air is the motive power that operates, through the action of thermostats, the steam valves on the radiators; the air is generated by 2 air compressors in the basement and is distributed by means of a network of piping to the different thermostats, and from these to the steam radiator valves. For this purpose about 120,000 feet of galvanized iron pipe of different sizes was used.

Nearly 1,200 thermostats are installed, and do their silent but efficient work for health, comfort and economy, operating more than 1,800 valves.

The valves on the skylight coils are operated by means of pneumatic push buttons.

The air used for this system is taken from the outside, compressed, then cooled and stored in tanks located in convenient cold places, and from there passes through the mains, risers and connections throughout the entire immense structure.

The advantage of temperature regulation is forcibly presented when it is taken into consideration that radiating surfaces must of necessity be of sufficient capacity to meet the requirements of the coldest weather, which occurs at short intervals during the winter season, and as a consequence it must follow that overheating will result unless the heating surfaces are thermostatically controlled.

THERE are about 1,600 steam radiators in the Singer Building. They have a superficial area of 66,234 square feet, or 1.52 acres. On a day with the temperature at zero, this surface will give out 17,883,180 heat units, equivalent to 537 H.P., which means the burning of one ton of coal per hour, if direct steam be used.

It is possible, however, to use exhaust steam from the engines and without appreciable "back pressure" to retard their action. This is accomplished by the Cryer Return Line System, which solves the problem of circulating exhaust steam for heating through such a large number of radiators and for such great distances without back pressure on the engines.

This system is very simple: it consists of a Cryer valve placed on the return end of each radiator, connecting into the return piping, on which a vacuum is maintained by means of vacuum pumps in the engine room. The water of condensation and the air are drawn freely through the Cryer valves to the vacuum pumps, which discharge to an air-separating tank, where the air is liberated and the water placed in condition to be again used in the boilers.

The Cryer valve holds the steam in the radiators until it is condensed, allowing only the water and air to pass into the return pipe, distinguishing absolutely between the three. It contains no springs, floats, or counterweights, or any parts requiring adjustment or attention. In fact, it has only one moving part, which is a heavy brass casting.

The use of this system permits a circulation through the radiators of exhaust steam, exhaust supplemented with live steam or live steam alone, without pressure. The radiators heat almost instantly when steam is turned on and stay hot as long as steam is supplied. The usual troubles due to leaky and faulty air valves are noticeably absent.

WEBSTER SYSTEM OF CIRCULATING STEAM FOR HEATING PURPOSES

THIS system was installed in the original Singer Building, corner of Broadway and Liberty Street, in 1898, or about two years after the erection of that building.

The purpose was to improve the gravity system originally erected with the building.

The Webster System proved so satisfactory in operation that it was adopted for the Bourne Building, erected in 1898. Improvements in details of the Webster apparatus since the original installation have been added and the Webster System is efficiently circulating the steam through all the radiators contained in the buildings named.

The Webster System is also used for heating the Singer factories at South Bend, Ind., and Elizabethport, N. J., also the Singer factories in Canada, Scotland and Germany, in all of which it has had a thorough test covering use during several seasons, and has demonstrated its efficiency in saving fuel and in improved heating conditions.

LIGHTING FIXTURES

THE lighting fixtures throughout all parts of the building were designed by Ernest Flagg, the architect, and executed by *The Enos Company* of New York City.

The designs in the main are simple, but of artistic merit, having the added and necessary attribute of being effective from a utilitarian standpoint. This basic idea governed even in the designs of the ornamental fixtures. There is no "straining for effect," and the whole lighting plan, while particularly inconspicuous as part of the general decorative scheme, produces the desired result—efficient and economical lighting—without introducing discordant features.

The design of the bracket illustrated was especially created for the main entrance corridor, in the style of the French Renaissance to which the decorative scheme of this part of the building conforms. The design commends itself in that it is particularly adapted to the location and also because the mechanical contrivances have been artistically concealed.

The lighting fixtures, excepting those in the main corridor, banking rooms and the Company's offices, are of the commercial type, of unconventional lines, particular care being given to their efficiency and structural strength in design and manufacture.

THERE are about 1,600 Kinnear Pressed Metal Steam Radiators in the Singer Building, all connected on the two-pipe vacuum return system.

Before they were adopted they were carefully tested as to their durability and efficiency by the owners and engineers of the Singer Building.

The Kinnear Radiators are manufactured by the Pressed Radiator Company, of Pittsburg, Pa., from decarbonized and dephosphorized metal, under their own specifications. The sheets, as they come from the mill, are No. 20 gauge, and are increased to 16 gauge by the galvanizing coating on the exterior and interior, which is obtained by complete immersion in molten spelter, which makes them impervious to rust and corrosion.

The amount of weight saved in this building by the installation of Kinnear Radiators instead of cast iron radiators is 309,500 lbs., or nearly 155 tons; the amount of floor space saved by their use is 1,310 square feet, an important factor in calculating rent values in the City of New York, were two of the points considered in the favor of these radiators.

The essential advantages in addition to the above, which the Kinnear Pressed Radiator possesses over the old style bulky cast iron radiator, is its quick response when placed in service. It heats instantly when steam is turned on, owing to the small amount of metal which must be heated before the radiator becomes an effective heating agent in the room. For the same reason, the radiator cools rapidly when the steam is turned off, thereby immediately stopping the heating effect in the room which it serves. The large amount of heat stored up and given off by the cast iron radiator after the steam is turned off frequently causes the occupant of a room to open the win-

dows wide, thereby causing dangerous draughts and excessive variations of temperature and, further, resulting in an undue waste of steam. This is an especially desirable feature when the Kinnear Pressed Radiators are used in connection with the automatic heat-controlling system which was installed in this building.

COAL TRACK, CRANE AND BLOCK EQUIPMENT

In the mechanical equipment is included a modern system for conveying coal from the vault to the boilers and for removing ashes from the ash pits to the elevator, by means of which they are raised to the sidewalk.

This system consists of an overhead carrying track extending through the coal vault and boiler room in front of the boilers, with a return track on the opposite side of the boiler room for handling the ashes. Each track is equipped with a standard track scale, allowing the coal to be weighed when it is brought from the coal vault and the ashes weighed before they are put on the elevator.

The particular style of apparatus was selected after the Architect and Consulting Engineers had inspected various systems already in use, and may be considered as the most modern method for handling coal and ashes.

In addition to the coal and ash handling system there was also installed a complete equipment of four 3-ton hand power traveling cranes and eighteen chain hoists and trolleys for handling field frames and armatures of the elevator machines, parts of the engines, generators, etc., in the engine room.

This equipment was furnished and installed complete in place by the *New Jersey Foundry & Machine Co.*, of 90 West Street, New York, who make a specialty of overhead handling systems and devices.

CROWN SANITARY FLOORING

AN important and novel feature in the Singer Building is the flooring used throughout its new portions. At first glance it appears to be linoleum, yet, after careful inspection, the bases around the walls and columns are found to be neatly joined by a coved connection, thus producing a continuous seamless floor and base.

This material is plastic when applied; it is spread upon the fireproof construction and carried up on the side wall to form a base. It is a beautiful red in color, and as the floor and base are in one sheet with a cove between them, there is no chance for dust and dirt to accumulate.

It is almost as noiseless as rubber, can be laid ½ inch thick over wood and can be readily cleansed by the usual means.

It was manufactured and applied by the *Robert A. Keasbey Co.* of New York City.

It is remarkable how evenly the work is executed, in view of the fact that many craftsmen were attending to their work about the building after the floors were installed.

To appreciate thoroughly the beauty of this flooring one should examine some of the offices occupied by the Singer Company. The simplicity of detail in these rooms is very charming, the greatest care having been exercised to bring out a harmonious effect between the wall colorings and the red floorings. This is especially true of the Directors' Room on the 34th floor. Not only these particular floors, but the offices throughout the Singer Addition, from the ground to the 39th floor; also the Liberty Street Extension, from the 8th to the 13th floor, are equipped with the Crown Flooring, more than 200,000 square feet having been laid in all.

When this immense floor space and the important part that it necessarily plays in the construction of the building are considered, it is only natural that a great sense of safety must be inspired in the tenants and those who continually use the building, in the fact that Crown Flooring, in addition to its solidity and strength when set in place, is absolutely fireproof. The finish of the floors is perhaps its most interesting feature in that the surface having been troweled to an absolute level, nearly approaches the hardness of slate without retaining any of the slippery qualities that usually go with a smooth, even surface. There is no doubt about the importance of the position in modern construction that a fireproof and sanitary floor, which at the same time permits of pleasing color schemes and absolute comfort combined with a lack of noise, must hold, and in the construction of this triumph in up-to-date building, the problem of the proper floor has been solved and perfection attained.

MODELING

THE modeling work for the many beautiful and intricate ornaments to be found throughout the Tower is deserving of particular praise.

The most striking examples are the two figures on the master-clock case in the main entrance corridor; the cartouches and caps of the marble columns, and the cartouches, brackets and other embellishments of this corridor. All this work is far above the realm of commercial art. The column cap cartouches are emblematical of the Singer Company's trade-mark, which has been interwoven with the architectural treatment in a very successful manner.

The most prominent external ornaments for which models were made, are the cartouches and brackets of the eight great arches near the top of the Tower; the urns, hip rolls and crestings on the dome, and the various ornaments on the lantern surmounting the latter. In addition, practically every ornament throughout the building had a model carefully prepared for it from the architect's full size detail drawing. These models were inspected and approved by the architect, after which the ornaments, whether of stone, copper, marble, iron, or bronze, were executed according to them.

The contract for all the modeling (excepting in plaster and terra cotta) was in the hands of *Henri J. Scheltgen & Co.*, Sculptors, Decorators and Modelers, No. 205 East Forty-fourth Street, New York.

PLASTERING

PLASTERING is the surface-forming part of interior architecture. It is the refined and finished work which completes the expression of the art of the architect. In the almost limitless wall areas it serves the ends of utility, while in the decorations and beautiful architectural enrichments its service is wholly ornamental. Ranging from the plain surfaces, either of plate glass smoothness, sand or stone finish, throughout all the various moldings, panelings, embellishments and decorative pieces of minute detail to the magnificent ornamental domes of the grand entrance corridor, it is the plastering that everywhere meets the eye of the owner, the tenant, and the visitor, and the impression is favorable, pleasing, or disturbing, according to the quality and perfection of the workmanship. The Singer Building has no more conspicuous or attractive feature than is found in the great work of the plain and decorative plastering.

H. W. Miller, Inc., executed all of the plain and ornamental plastering of the Singer Building. The highest class and finest quality of materials were used in every part of the work. Mechanics of long experience and special skill were employed to do the work. A selected staff of French and German expert modelers and artists put into lasting form the beautiful decorative and ornamental designs of the architect. The work was begun in November, 1907, and was completed in June, 1908.

The hard setting base, or first coating, amounted in area to 700,000 feet, and over 5,000,000 pounds of prepared King's Windsor Cement Plastering were used in the work. Upward of 200 tons of other materials were used in the various finishing coats, such as Keene's Cement, Portland Cement and Rockland-Rockport Lime. The cement base is 8 miles in length and there are 2 miles of molded cornice in the corridors.

The partitions and furred walls of this great building required 256,000 square feet of metal laths, to support which were used 50 miles of structural angle iron, 130 miles of wire and 110,000 bolts. The metal beading, used to protect the corners, if laid in a straight line would extend over 155,000 feet, or nearly 30 miles.

Hundreds of barrels and 50,000 bags were required to hold the great mass of plastering material while being transported to the building, and the days' time of the skilled workmen employed in the execution of the work and paid at the rate of $5.50 for the eight-hour day, amounted to seventeen years.

The accompanying illustration is a photograph of a portion of the arched and domed ceiling of the main entrance corridor. There are nineteen of these great ornamental plaster domes resting upon decorative plaster arches, supported by square marble columns with bronze capitals and bronze moldings; the columns being 12 feet from center to center each way. The decorative arches and ornamental domes were executed in the style of the French Renaissance, and are rich in detail and artistic embellishment. The grouping of the stately columns, the artistic taste and rare beauty of the ornamentation, and the perfection and refinement of the molded plaster arches and domes make this grand corridor unquestionably the most beautiful and impressive ever erected in a great commercial building in the City of New York.

Another notable portion of the plastering is to be found in the basement corridor leading to the heavy armor-plate Safe Deposit Vaults. The finish here is in artificial Caen Stone, of a soft, yellowish gray tint. The work comprises massive columns, 14 feet in circumference, paneled walls and arched and domed ceilings. Artificial Caen Stone is an imported French material, closely resembling the natural stone, to which it is superior because of its hardness. The work throughout gives the effect of massiveness and stability.

Another conspicuous portion of the plastering work occurs in the principal offices of The Singer Manufacturing Company, comprising the 33d, 34th and 35th stories of the building. Here are ornamental plaster cornices, ornamental paneled ceilings in plaster and ornamental paneled walls in Keene's Cement, all molded and executed from special designs by the architect.

The work is not elaborate in detail, but substantial and dignified in effect, and well adapted to the purpose—that is, the decoration and ornamentation of the offices of a great manufacturing company.

The members of *H. W. Miller, Inc.*, and the skilled mechanics and artists employed by them, all heartily joined with the architect and owners in a harmonious effort to reach the desired result—a completed piece of work of the highest excellence, made of the most reliable and enduring materials and executed in the most skillful and artistic manner known to the trade.

[68]

ARCHED AND DOMED CEILING OF MAIN CORRIDOR

PAINTING

INTERIOR WALL FINISH

THE finish used on the walls of all halls, corridors and stair wells throughout the Singer Building and Tower is "Satinette," which, to harmonize more perfectly with the rest of the decorative scheme, was in this instance tinted a light cream.

In its original manufactured state "Satinette" is a pure white material, accomplishing by distinctive means the ideals that decorators have heretofore sought to attain by the use of enamels and the more primitive pigment and gloss combinations. Its history, if published in full, would be far from dull reading. *Pinchin, Johnson & Co., Ltd.,* the veteran London house in whose laboratories it originated, had been working on various formulas more than ten years before making the discovery which started their chemists on a new line of experimenting that led, by an extremely original and ingenious course, to the desired end.

The announcement that, by scientific means, a perfect white had been given absolute permanency and rendered invulnerable against repeated washing created wide interest in Great Britain and throughout Europe. The material was adopted with a readiness and prevalence quite unprecedented. Spain and the south of France embraced it almost as early as did England and Scotland; it was being applied in the Monte Carlo casinos before it was fairly dry in the ballrooms of London hotels.

In America the Singer Company was the first to take it up for extensive use as a washable finish, others having employed it only decoratively. It was applied not alone on the interior, but on the exteriors of the court walls, thus accomplishing both beautiful tone within and exceptional light effect without.

All purchases of the material were made of *Pinchin, Johnson & Co.'s* American licensee, the *Standard Var-nish Works,* through its central office at No. 29 Broadway, New York, and an idea of the amount used can be formed from the statement that it was an equivalent to what would be necessary to single-coat an area of nearly five acres, or a strip 1 foot wide completely around the Island of Manhattan—40 miles. This, notwithstanding the fact that the covering capacity was so much greater than had been anticipated that the amount consumed was 30 per cent. less than the decorator's estimate based upon the average enamel covering capacity.

EXTERIOR AND INTERIOR PAINTING

PAINTING the exterior of the Singer Tower was the most hazardous work on the building, because the painters worked on swinging scaffolds ranging from 100 to 600 feet above the ground.

This work was conducted to a satisfactory conclusion without accident or mishap. The scope of the work included painting all metal work, both interior and exterior, finishing all new and refinishing all hard wood, painting and enameling all elevator shafts and toilet rooms, and painting exterior brick work of the courts. This work was done by the *W. P. Nelson Co.*, No. 120 West Twenty-ninth Street, New York.

Among the many new problems met with, and successfully solved, in the erection of the Singer Tower, not the least was

USE OF "VITRALITE" FOR CERTAIN SURFACES to secure a permanent, durable coating for those wall surfaces that are subject to unusually severe conditions and, on account of their location, demand special consideration with respect to sanitary properties.

The floors generally, throughout this building, are left free of partitions, being planned in the nature of lofts, and subdivided with temporary partitions, according to the wishes and needs of the tenants.

The permanent partitions are those forming the toilet rooms and lavatories. These toilet rooms and lavatories occur on every floor. In all of them the walls and ceilings were covered with the English enamel "Vitralite," made by *Robert Ingham Clark & Co., Ltd.*, London, England, associated with *Pratt & Lambert*, New York, from whom this enamel was purchased.

As these surfaces require frequent and thorough cleansing, and as there is always a considerable amount of moisture in places of this character, "Vitralite" enamel was selected on account of its great durability. For the same reason it is used on the entire surface of the immense elevator shafts, at present the highest in existence. For these purposes over 500 gallons of the "Vitralite" enamel were applied by the *W. P. Nelson Co.*, under the supervision of the architect.

INTERIOR DECORATING

ALL the walls and ceilings throughout the Singer Tower are decorated up to and including the 13th story. The ceilings are done in white water color and the walls painted a light tan shade to harmonize with the trim finished in oak.

Above the 13th story, throughout the entire upper office portion of the Tower, the ceilings are painted a light ivory color, while the walls are a dainty shade of green that blends admirably with the metal trim, doors, etc., which are finished in mahogany color.

The ceilings of the corridors in the Tower, likewise in the Singer Building, Bourne Building and Bourne Building Addition, are painted white and the walls a light cream shade, finished with two coats of enamel.

The decorations on the ceiling of the main entrance form the most striking feature of this contract. Here gold leaf to the value of many hundreds of dollars is applied with great skill and discrimination to bring out the beautiful and intricate ornamentations in the series of vaults and domes surmounting the marble columns. Especially at night, when this corridor remains illuminated while the rest of the building is in darkness, it appears to the beholder like the nave of some wonderful, golden cathedral.

An idea of the magnitude of this decorating contract may be obtained from the statement that more than 4,500 gallons of material were required; and while the employment of from 100 to 200 artisans resulted in the completion of the entire work within the specified time limit of thirty days, it would have taken more than nine years' constant labor on the part of one man to finish the task. Moreover, it is seldom that so large a contract for painting and decorating is completed in so short a time without the registering of a single complaint or criticism. The entire work, as described, was executed by *William F. Margerin,* No. 358 West Forty-second Street, New York.

LOOKING NORTH FROM THE SINGER TOWER

HARDWARE

THE Singer Building is equipped, throughout, with "Russwin Hardware," furnished by *Russell & Erwin Manufacturing Co.*, Contract Department, No. 26 West Twenty-sixth Street, New York City; factories at New Britain, Conn.

The "Russwin Unit Lock" represents the high-est development in the art of modern lock-making. It is especially adapted to office buildings, simplicity of construction and ease of application being two of its principal features.

The "Russwin Liquid Door Check" has proved its superiority by perfect operation under the most severe conditions to which any check has been sub-jected. The door checks in the Singer Tower are located at a greater altitude than any heretofore in use.

[73]

THE DIRECTORS' ROOM

OFFICE FURNITURE

THE Executive Offices of The Singer Manufacturing Company, covering the entire 34th floor of the Singer Building, are equipped throughout with mahogany furniture manufactured by the *Doten-Dunton Desk Co.* of New York and Boston.

The furniture shown in the appended illustration of the Directors' Room is uniform in every detail of design, material, construction and finish, and each piece bears its relation to and architecturally conforms with every other.

It is made throughout of selected Honduras mahogany, and the cabinet work, veneering, carving, etc., is of the highest grade. We mention the following special features:

Drawers, hand dovetailed. Drawer bottoms of three-ply Figured Mahogany. Drawer sides and backs of Figured Mahogany. Solid Division between each two Drawers making separate Dust-proof Compartments. Veneers (except where branch veneers are used) are one quarter inch thick. Branch Veneer panels mitered at center on Davenports, Chairs, Tables and Bookcases.

Such furniture appeals to the discriminating man and creates the right impression upon all who see it.

ELECTRIC CLOCK SYSTEM

THE "Magneta" Electric Clock System, manufactured by the *Magneta Clock Company*, Nos. 120 and 122 West Thirty-first Street, New York, the latest and most up-to-date electric time-clock system on the market, has been installed throughout the Singer Building.

Batteries and contact-points, which have been the cause of much dissatisfaction and trouble in other electric clock systems, in this have been entirely eliminated.

The entire system of secondary clocks throughout the building is actuated by the master-clock shown in the illustration. This is located in an ornamental bronze casing in the main corridor.

The winding of the master-clock is done by an electric motor, which obtains the necessary current from the electric plant in the building and winds up the weight automatically once every day.

The weight operates the clock movement proper, as well as the current-producing magneto apparatus. The magneto apparatus is released every half minute, thus generating a positive and strong current, and operating the secondary clocks throughout the building.

To insure absolute correctness of time, the master-clock is equipped with a "Remonitoir" escapement, such as is used on the finest astronomical regulators and tower clocks, where accurate timekeeping is desired. It is also equipped with an Invar Steel Pendulum; a pendulum which has given far better results than the mercurial pendulums.

The secondary clocks are connected in series.

All wire is heavy rubber covered, and is run through a separate conduit system, thus avoiding interference with other wires.

METAL TRIM

IN view of the recent revisions of the building codes in most large cities, it is interesting to note the improvements in building construction made to comply with the demands for better fire protection.

The Singer Building is notable in this respect; the visitor's attention is immediately claimed by the uniform color and beautiful grain of the interior trim, and it is only upon a very close and careful examination that the nature of this trim is revealed. Steel again proves its great commercial value, for this is the composition of what are to all appearances oak and mahogany doors, partitions, moldings, etc.

The æsthetic appearance and the faithful carrying out of design and graining in what appears to be re-markably fine woodwork is truly wonderful, and a brief description of its manufacture and erection will be noted with interest. The stiles, rails and mullions of the steel doors in the Singer Building are hollow except for a cork filler used to deaden the sound.

Possibly the most important feature in the manufacture of these doors and of similar sheet steel construction, is the perfected process used to draw cold steel through dies rather than the common method of rolling it while hot, the latter method being usual for large and heavy sections. The first-mentioned process enables sharp, well-defined angles and well-rounded curves in the molding, thus imposing on the designer practically no limitation of ideas.

COLD DRAWN STEEL

The making of the draw dies for the production of sheet steel moldings requires a well-adapted tool room to meet the many possible requirements arising in the adoption of this material for building purposes.

Dies having been made and perfected fully to interpret the ideas of the designer, the moldings are drawn out in lengths of from 30 to 50 feet. They are then cut into required lengths and sent to the press room to be notched and drilled for connections.

In the formation of hollow steel doors the first operation is to trim large sheets of patent leveled steel to exact sizes.

FIRST FORMATION

Particular care must be taken in this operation as the variation from plan of the 64th part of an inch will cause an imperfect result. This done, the moldings are formed in the sheets, openings are cut for hardware and the proper bends made.

A peculiar feature of hollow steel door-making will here be noticed; i. e., that the size and nature of hardware must be taken into account at the very inception instead of at the completion of the door, as in the case of either Kalamein or wood doors. The partly formed sheets of steel are then sent to the paint shop to be completely covered by a protective coat of oil paint.

From the press and machine rooms the various parts, after having been coated, are

ASSEMBLING AND FITTING

placed in the assembly room, where the mechanical perfection of the door and trim is attained. Here the parts are so closely fitted as to secure invisible joints, a result most important if a pleasing effect is to be produced and dust pockets are to be avoided.

In the finishing department the door receives special preparation and goes through various processes to insure a smooth surface before the paint is applied. This includes the baking of the door in specially constructed ovens, in order to obtain an

ENAMELING

adhesion of the prime coat to the steel so that it will not crack under the blows of the hammer or the bending, expansion or contraction of the metal. The body coat of paint is now applied and treated by special processes, in-

cluding baking, rubbing, etc., and the door is then turned over to the artist for graining.

The appearance of the steel doors and partitions in the Singer Building is so true to nature in showing the beautiful grain of carefully se-

ARTISTIC FINISH

lected, well-finished quartered oak and Honduras mahogany as to deceive experts into the belief that these woods were used. This is produced by artistic hand-graining on the surface of the metal sheet, prepared as has been described. The door is then varnished, baked and rubbed, and is finished, so far as the factory operations are concerned.

Having the mechanical and æsthetic features fully developed, it may be well to consider the erection of the work and how it compares with that of other material. The door can be placed in a building many weeks earlier than a wooden door, for there is no fear of its swelling or warping, due to dampness; as soon as erected it immediately comes into

ERECTING THE WORK efficient service, an advantage often of the utmost importance. The dangers of marring the door are slight, because the enamel is baked on so thoroughly that blows, due to carelessness of workmen, do not readily mar the finish as they would that of a wooden door. The finish being complete before the work leaves the factory, the necessity of finishing on the job, where there is exposure to dust, is entirely obviated.

The door jamb and casing are fastened directly to rolled iron channels or angles placed in the openings before plastering, or wooden "bucks" fastened to these channels may be used and the door jambs fastened thereto. The wooden "bucks" are completely covered by the steel jamb and casing, and the door hinges are fastened to the iron channel with machine screws, thus obviating the dependence upon the wood to bear the strain of the weight of the door. The advantage of this latter method is apparent.

The doors can be erected much faster than wooden doors, as all measurements are exact and once in place there is no necessity for rehanging, due to swelling or other causes.

The visitor will notice a large number of steel partitions, picture moldings, window trim, corridor **VARIETY OF STEEL TRIM** lights, wainscoting, cap and many other items required for the complete interior equipment of this modern building. The methods of manufacture in each case are almost identical with those described. It is well to note the features introduced in the steel partitions, whereby they can be quickly taken down and reërected in any desired part of the building. Variations in lengths and heights are taken up by adjustment provided for in the "filler" pieces on the sides and top. All of the sheet metal doors, partitions, and trim in the Singer Building were made and erected into place by the *Dahlstrom Metallic Door Company*, of Jamestown, N. Y. New York office at No. 299 Broadway. The paneled steel wainscoting on the 34th floor, shown in the accompanying illustration, is worthy of notice as it produces a remarkably cozy effect in the room.

ADVANTAGES OF STEEL TRIM Briefly stated, the advantages gained by the use of doors, partitions, trim, etc., of the Dahlstrom System are: fireproofness, dispatch in completion of the building, uniformity of design and color, durability and utility.

SAFETY DEVICE FOR WINDOW CLEANERS

THE Whitner Safety Device for outside window cleaners, as attached to the Singer Building, consists of bronze bolts screwed into the metal window casings, two on a side. The window cleaner wears a regulation belt, made in the usual fashion, of heavy frames, fourfold and double stitched, provided with aluminum bronze terminals and brass rope eyes. The window cleaner raises the window, attaches one of the terminals to the belt, steps out upon the window ledge, attaches the other terminal and is securely fastened to the building, with no possibility of falling, both hands being left free to work with. The belt is so constructed that he is permitted to move from one side of the window to the other.

Ten years ago it was difficult to convince architects and builders that it was necessary to protect out-

side window cleaners, an occupation made extra hazardous by the height of the modern skyscraper. To-day, however, the Whitner Safety Device is recognized as a "necessary modern improvement," and is found on up-to-date buildings in all parts of the country.

It is claimed that there has never been an accident where the Whitner Safety Device was used.

The home office of the *Whitner Safety Device Co.* is at Chicago, Ill.; the New York office is at No. 2 Rector Street.

THE MECHANICAL PLANT

THE MECHANICAL PLANT—INTRODUCTORY

OFFICE OF THE CHIEF ENGINEER OF THE SINGER BUILDING

BEFORE the present alterations and additions were made, the plant of the old Singer and Bourne Buildings consisted principally of four Babcock & Wilcox water-tube boilers aggregating 546 H. P., and seven Diehl generators, of a total capacity of 387.5 kilowatts, direct-connected to six Ball & Wood engines of 572 indicated H. P. There were further three 10-in. x 6-in. x 10-in. house-service and fire pumps, the usual complement of boiler-feed and return pumps; three feed-water heaters; pumps, tanks and motors for three hydraulic and three electrical elevators; a 2½-ton refrigerating plant; a 10 H. P. vacuum sweeping plant; vacuum return pumps and tanks, air compressors, filters, grease extractors, separators and other similar appurtenances.

Roughly speaking, this plant occupied the westerly half of the basement of the old Singer Building and the easterly half of the basement of the adjoining Bourne Building, the boilers being located in the forward part of these spaces.

After careful consideration it was found that the owners' interests would be best served by replacing this entire equipment with a new plant of ample capacity to take care of the remodeled and greatly enlarged group of buildings. But it was necessary to accomplish this transformation gradually, according to a carefully prearranged programme, for while the change was being made the Singer and Bourne Buildings had to be supplied uninterruptedly with heat, light, water and elevator service, and the new buildings with temporary heat and light.

The new boiler plant, consisting of five Babcock & Wilcox water-tube boilers, aggregating about 2,000 H. P., was therefore installed first, and located in the basement of the Bourne Addition Building about 60 feet west of the old engine room and connected to it by means of a pipe passage, as indicated on the accompanying plan.

These boilers are equipped with superheaters and a balanced draft system, the blower of which is located north of boiler No. 5, as shown.

From this blower, indicated by the number 8 on the boiler-room plan, is run the main balanced draft duct (marked 10) at the rear of the boilers, with a number of branch ducts extending to the bridge wall of each boiler, as indicated by the dotted lines. The advantages of this balanced draft system are described in detail farther on; incidentally, it helps to keep down the temperature of the boiler room, which is one of the coolest in the city.

There is an overhead smoke breeching at the rear of the boilers, marked 6 on the plan, extending to the steel smokestack, marked 7, located in the northwest corner of the building. An air space has been left around the stack, between it and the surrounding brickwork, from the basement to the roof, for ventilating the boiler room.

Above the roof the stack has been carried over to the north and combined with that of the City Investing Building, an unusual procedure, never before attempted, as far as the writer knows. The results have been very satisfactory.

There are installed in the new boiler room two feed pumps; a feed-water meter; a blow-off tank located in a sump, with electrical drain pump; an overhead coal trolley with scales; a ventilating blower, and underground vacuum ash conveyer pipes.

These, marked 21 on the plan, consist of a main, extra-heavy wrought iron pipe, with branches extending to a series of cast iron boxes, with removable strainer covers. There are three of these located in the floor just in front of each boiler, so that the ashes may be raked directly into them; and one between each pair of boilers, for drawing off the soot at the side clean-out doors.

The new boiler room is connected to the engine room by means of a 12-inch high-pressure steam main, extending from the rear of the boilers through the pipe gallery to the engine room, along the westerly wall of the latter (where the connections to the new engines are taken off), thence to the front of the building and back to the boiler room, thus making a complete circuit.

This main is marked 22 on the plan.

Parallel to the 12-inch main over the boilers is located a 6-inch auxiliary main. This is likewise run through the pipe gallery to the engine room and

branches to the pumps, compressors, heating main and various minor appurtenances.

After the new boiler plant had been placed in commission the old boilers were removed, thereby making room for one of the new engines and generators and the new pumping plant. At the same time the erection of an extension at the rear of the Bourne Building afforded opportunity for installing another of the new engine-generator units. In this manner the old units were gradually replaced.

The new power plant consists of five units composed of three simple and two compound Ball & Wood engines, coupled with Diehl generators, aggregating 1,400 kilowatts' capacity. A detailed description of them will be found in succeeding pages. They occupy the entire space of what was originally the Bourne Building engine and boiler room, with a rear extension. Four of them are placed in a straight line, leaving a large open space in front of the main switch board, as will be seen by referring to the plan. Opposite the switch board is placed the steam-gauge board. A generous amount of space is left around each unit; as a result the building has one of the most imposing engine rooms in the city.

The engine and generator foundations are built of armored concrete, designed, with considerable ingenuity, so as to avoid the old grillage foundations under the columns of the Bourne Building.

The leads from the generators to the switch board consist of lead armored cables in underground iron conduits.

Each steam connection from the 12-inch main to the engines is equipped with a steam separator to insure the delivery of dry steam. These separators are described in detail farther on. A 10-inch and an 18-inch exhaust main are run under the engine-room floor, east of the engines, with an underground connection to each. These two mains are combined into a 20-inch pipe marked 26 on the plan, from which a branch was passed through the feed-water heater, located in the pump room, east of the engine room. In this heater a portion of the exhaust steam is utilized for heating the boiler feed water, which is pumped through it from the suction tanks to the boilers by the boiler-feed pumps.

The 20-inch exhaust main is run in the form of a loop around the feed-water heater, as shown on the plan. From this loop are taken the principal heating mains. Should, for any reason, the supply of exhaust steam become inadequate for heating purposes, live steam may be injected into the exhaust loop through a 6-inch high-pressure steam connection, after reducing the steam pressure from 160 pounds down to

ONE END OF THE MACHINE SHOP, SINGER BUILDING

about 1 pound, or even atmospheric pressure, by means of the pressure-reducing valve which is mounted on the 6-inch connection.

After the various heating mains were supplied from it, the 20-inch exhaust main was fitted with a back-pressure valve (to maintain the pressure in the exhaust piping required for heating purposes) and then extended from a point above engine No. 2 up to the roof of the Bourne Building. Here it was run over to the roof of the Bourne Building Addition to get it as far away from the Tower as possible and finally capped with a cast iron exhaust head.

The engine room is equipped with a complete system of overhead I-beam tracks and trolleys with chain blocks, for handling valves or parts of the engines and generators. It is cooled by air delivered at numerous points along the ceiling through galvanized iron ducts connected with electrically driven

blowers located in the fan room, east of the switch board. This air is previously filtered, washed and tempered in an elaborately constructed intake, located over engine No. 5.

Like the engine room, the various elevator machinery rooms throughout the building have been equipped with overhead tracks, traveling cranes, trolleys, and chain blocks for handling parts of their machinery in case of a breakdown. Spare armatures mounted on trucks, are conveniently stored for immediately replacing any that may burn out, thus guarding against protracted interruptions of the elevator service.

East of the engine room, in the basement of the old Singer Building, is now located the pump room, repair shop and Chief Engineer's office.

There is also an electrician's room and a waste-paper room, containing a press, by means of which all the waste paper, gathered up daily throughout the building, is baled and then disposed of. The paper is sent down into this room through a chute.

In the pump room is placed the feed-water heater above mentioned; a 20-ton compression system refrigerating plant, and the six principal pumps, of Worthington make. Two of these are installed for the fire service, two for the low-pressure and two for the high-pressure house services. For the details of these services the reader is referred to the chapter on Plumbing.

The fire pumps are of the horizontal duplex, direct acting steam type, each having a capacity of not less than 500 gallons per minute against a pressure of 300 pounds, when operating at a piston speed not exceeding 100 feet per minute.

The low-pressure house pumps are of the compound direct acting, duplex steam type, of 200 gallons capacity per minute against 100 pounds pressure, 66 feet piston speed; the high-pressure pumps are of similar type of 120 gallons capacity against 300 pounds 50 feet piston speed. They are brass fitted throughout and their cylinders lagged in the customary manner.

The pump room further contains the "low-tension" motor generators, for furnishing current to bells, phonographs and similar services, which are usually run by batteries in smaller plants; also the "low-tension" switch board. This service is more fully described in another chapter.

The office of the Chief Engineer, Mr. J. C. Buxton, is a commodious room, 14 x 20 ft., completely equipped with bookcases and draughting tables; a telephone central station connecting with all parts of the mechanical and elevator plant; pressure and recording gauges; controlling valves of the Foster Automatic Valve System for emergency purposes, and the electrical position indicator board of the elevator service.

The entrance door to the entire mechanical plant is under the control of the chief engineer's office, which must be passed by all visitors to the engine room.

The space at the rear of the main switch board was utilized for the New York Telephone Company's board, and for the pump, pressure and discharge tanks of the Otis Company's hydraulic sidewalk lifts.

Adjoining the engine room on the northeast is located the compressor room. Here are two Ingersoll-Rand 8-in., 13-in., 12-in., and 7½-in., x 10-in. compound steam and air Imperial "Type Ten" Air Compressors, with 45-inch fly-wheels, having a capacity of 210 cubic feet of free air per minute, at 160 revolutions and developing 37 indicated H. P.

A compressed air system has been installed, consisting substantially of a 30-inch by 72-inch tank and a 2-inch air main extending to the boiler room, with outlets and hose for cleaning the boilers; further, of a header in the engine room, with outlets at each generator, and of branches to the several banks of elevators, elevator motors, ventilating fans and circulating pumps, all for cleaning purposes.

The compressor room also contains the machines and separators of the Vacuum Cleaner System, more fully described under that heading; the hot-water service heaters; some parts of the refrigerating plant; the ice-water circulating pumps; the automatic oiling system and various minor fixtures.

A description of the ice- and hot-water services will be found under Plumbing.

Above the compressor room is located the filter and tank room, readily reached from the engine room by means of an iron stairway. Here are placed the Scaife water filters and the suction tanks, into which all the water is delivered from the street mains and thence pumped to the various parts of the building.

All high-pressure steam piping is of extra heavy wrought iron; changes in directions and connections to engines and pumps are made with long sweep pipe bends having welded flanges.

All fittings 2½-inch and over are flanged and all designed for 250 pounds working pressure, although 160 pounds is the pressure now carried. The work is thoroughly covered with 85 per cent. carbonate of magnesia throughout, three thicknesses being used on practically all of the high-pressure piping.

All high-pressure steam piping is drained by means of the Holly Return System and protected by the Foster Automatic non-return combination valves.

Insulated ceilings are erected over the boiler and engine rooms, concealing, in the latter, a good many of the minor conduits and pipes, but leaving them accessible through manholes and similar openings.

The toilet, shower-bath and locker accommodations for both the boiler and engine rooms are in keeping with the high character of all the appointments.

The floors of the engine room and adjoining rooms are finished in red tile throughout. The trench covers have been inlaid with the same material. The walls, including those of the boiler room, are lined with white enameled brick and tile. This treatment, in combination with the polished brasswork and the dark green finish of the engines, generators and other fixtures, has resulted in a very agreeable effect.

In a word, everything has been done to give the mechanical plant a setting commensurate with its importance and the large part which it is called upon to play in the successful maintenance of the building and the comfort and convenience of its occupants.

KEY TO PLANS OF BOILER ROOM AND MECHANICAL PLANT

1–5.—Boilers.
6.—Smoke Breeching.
7.—Boiler Flue.
8.—Balanced Draft Blower.
9.—Balanced Draft-Blower Engine.
10.—Balanced Draft Duct.
11.—Feed-Water Heater.
12–13.—Boiler-Feed Pumps.
14.—Blow-off Tank.
15.—Blow-off Pump.
16.—Holly Receiver.
17.—Sump and Sump Pump.
18.—Ventilating Blower.
19.—Ventilating Blower Motor.
20.—Coal Trolley.
21.—Pneumatic Ash-Conveyor Pipes.
22.—High-Pressure Steam Main.
23.—Auxiliary Steam Main.
24.—Sidewalk Lift.
25.—Coal Scales.
26.—Exhaust Main.
27.—Exhaust to Roof.
28.—Pressure-Reducing Valve.
29.—Back-Pressure Valve.
30.—Heating Mains.
31.—Exhaust Piping.
32.—Feed-Water Heater.
33.—Engine No. 1.
34.—Generator No. 1.
35.—Engine No. 2.
36.—Generator No. 2.
37.—Engine No. 3.
38.—Generator No. 3.
39.—Engine No. 4.
40.—Generator No. 4.
41.—Engine No. 5.
42.—Generator No. 5.
43.—Steam Separators.
44.—Main Switch Board.
45.—Gauge Board.
46.—Telephone Company's Board.
47.—Electrical Pump for Sidewalk Lifts.
48.—Auxiliary Steam Pump for Sidewalk Lifts.
49.—Tanks for Sidewalk Lifts.
50.—Oil Pumps.
51.—Fresh-Air Blowers.
52.—Elevators.
53–54.—Fire Pumps.
55–56.—Low-Pressure House Pumps.
57–58.—High-Pressure House Pumps.
59.—Hot-Water Service Heaters.
60.—Ice-Water Circulating Pumps.
61.—Ice-Water Filters.
62.—Condenser.
63.—Ice Machine.
64.—Freezing Tank.
65.—Can Dump.
66.—Ice-Water Storage Tank.
67.—Ice-Water Circulating Pump.
68–69.—Vacuum Pumps.
70.—Low-Tension Motor Generator.
71.—Low-Tension Switch Boards.
72.—Electrical Elevator Position Indicator.
73.—Gauge Board.
74.—Telephone Board.
75.—Emery Wheels.
76.—Hacksaw.
77.—Drill.
78.—Lathes.
79.—Grinding Machine.
80.—Shaking Machine.
81.—Pipe-Bending Machine.
82.—Idler.
83.—Motor.
84.—Lockers.
85–86.—Air Compressors.
87.—Air Compressor Tank.
88, 89, 90.—Vacuum Cleaner Pumps.
91.—Vacuum Cleaner Separator Tanks.
92.—Vacuum Pumps for Drips.
93.—Discharge Tank.
94.—Thermostatic Pumps.
95.—Motor.
96.—Filter.
97.—Pump Governor.

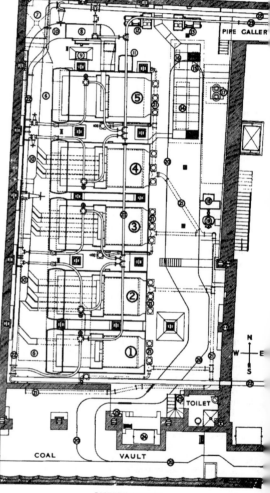

LIBERTY STREET

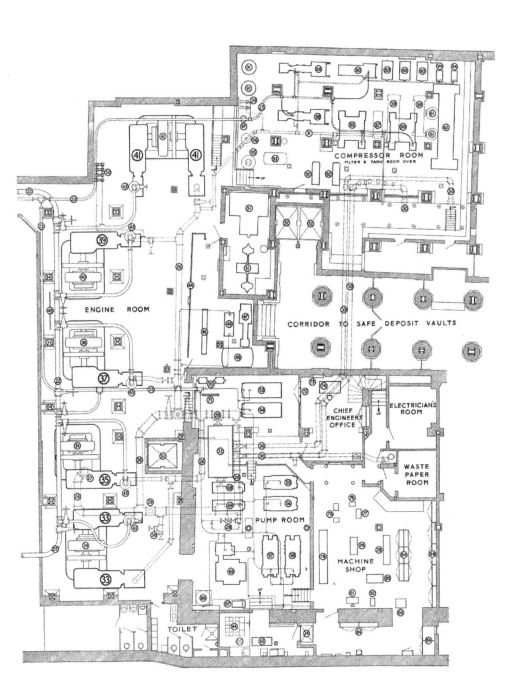

BOILERS

VERY few realize either the important part which steam plays in the maintenance and operation of office buildings or the vast quantity of energy which is daily generated by the combustion of coal and through the peculiar properties of steam safely and economically stored and utilized as required in the various mechanical processes necessary for the transportation and conveniences of this great commercial center.

Since steam was first utilized as a means of storing and conveying the heat energy developed by the combustion of coal and other fuels, there has been a gradual development and evolution of the steam

boiler from the time of Hero until to-day. Its removal from the chain of useful mechanical appliances would be followed by a complete paralysis of the world's present material prosperity and activity and, until some other means of storing and distributing energy had been developed, an almost total paralysis of commerce.

In the earlier days steam was utilized at low pressures of only a few pounds above the atmosphere. Finding that an increase in pressure was accompanied by an increase in the amount of work that could be done per pound of fuel consumed, boiler makers gradually changed their designs, until to-day the latest developments of water-tube boilers make available 150 to 200 pounds in stationary and up to 300 pounds' pressure per square inch in marine service. Sufficient energy is stored in one of the old-fashioned plain cylindrical boilers at 100 pounds' steam pressure to project it to a height of over $3\frac{1}{2}$ miles.

A cubic foot of heated water in an ordinary boiler carrying 70 pounds of steam pressure has about the same explosive energy as a pound of gunpowder. That some forms of boilers in use to-day do explode, is witnessed by the sad list of casualties from this cause every year—in fact almost daily.

It is now fully established by the experience of Boiler Insurance Associations in this country and England, that all of the mystery of boiler explosions consists in a want of sufficient strength to withstand the pressure. This lack of strength may be inherent in the original design and construction, but it is most frequently the effect of weakening of iron and steel by strains due to unequal expansion caused by unequal heating of different parts of the boiler, or it may be due to corrosion from long use or improper care.

The first element of safety is ample strength, which can be best attained in connection with thin heating surface by small diameters of parts under pressure.

The second element of safety is the prevention of strains from expansion or other forces by providing the necessary elasticity.

The third element of safety is such an arrangement of parts that when, through gross carelessness or oversight, the water becomes low and the boiler overheated, a rupture, if it occur, shall be localized and of so small a detail that no serious disaster can follow.

In addition to being safe, a boiler must be economical and durable. To be economical the heating surface must be so disposed that the maximum amount of heat shall be absorbed from the heated products of combustion by the water in the boiler.

To be durable, all parts of the boiler must be readily accessible for inspection and cleaning, and must be so assembled and of such material as to be free from excessive strains and deterioration incidental to the various extremes of temperature and to the chemical constituents of the gases and water, which are necessarily characteristic of the process of steam generation.

With the essential properties of a steam boiler,

safety, economy and durability, always in mind, *The Babcock & Wilcox Company*, striving to turn out the best boiler that money could buy, have during the last quarter of a century developed and perfected the Babcock & Wilcox Water-Tube Boiler.

That the tubular sectional principle of construction, its distinguishing feature, fulfills the require-

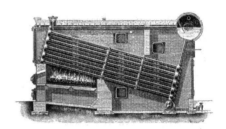

ments of safety has been demonstrated by the fact that there are nearly 6,000,000 H.P. of Babcock & Wilcox boilers in use.

That they are durable, is witnessed by the fact that practically every Babcock & Wilcox boiler which has been built during the past twenty-five years is in use to-day carrying the steam pressure for which it was designed.

That they are efficient, is at least indicated by the fact that the entire electric transportation system of the City of Greater New York, including surface, elevated, and subway railroads, the electric service of the New York Central and of the New York, New Haven & Hartford Railroads are all operated from central power stations equipped only with the product of The Babcock & Wilcox Company, as are all of the central stations of the New York Edison Company, which controls the distribution of electric light and power in this city.

In the basement of the Singer Building there are installed five Babcock & Wilcox sectional water-tube boilers, four having a nominal rating of 400 H.P. each and one having a nominal rating of 325 H.P., or a total of 1,925 H.P. They can in case of necessity supply and continuously develop 2,888 H.P. These boilers furnish all of the power required for the operation of the elevators and the various apparatus incidental to the maintenance and operation of this great building.

DUMPING GRATES

THERE were four sets of Thompson dumping grates in use under the boilers in the old Singer plant for almost five years.

This fact caused the adoption of the same make of grates for the furnaces of the five large Babcock & Wilcox boilers in the new Singer Building.

One of these furnaces is 7 feet, 4 inches wide and 9 feet long. The four others are each 9 feet square, making a total of 390 square feet of grates.

The Thompson grate is especially designed and adapted for burning the finer grades of fuel, such as pea coal, Numbers 1, 2 and 3 buckwheat, screenings, etc. It is fitted up on a very substantial frame with adjustable legs, and is independent of all brick work.

The frames and rockers are not subject to intense heat, and are practically indestructible. The grates are interchangeable.

The illustration represents a set of Thompson dumping grates as installed in one of the 9 x 9 foot furnaces, with the two front sections of right side dumped. They are made with ¼-inch air space and burn No. 2 buckwheat coal. They are operated in nine sections, three in width and three in length. To clean the fire, the ashpit doors are partly closed, the live coal pushed back from the two front sections, which are connected and dumped together, then the coal is drawn forward and the back section dumped, the coal then spread and fired up; the same operation is performed on each section, and the entire furnace is thoroughly cleaned and fired up in from four to five minutes without waste of coal and but slight drop in steam pressure; the ashes and clinkers are then wetted down and taken out at leisure, all dust being avoided.

These grates were made and installed by *Richard Thompson & Co.*, No. 126 Liberty Street, New York.

THE BALANCED DRAFT SYSTEM OF FURNACE REGULATION

IT is a noteworthy fact that many of the modern skyscraper office buildings, as well as the big industrial steam plants and power houses throughout the country, are equipped with the Balanced Draft System of Furnace Regulation, under patents owned by *The Engineer Company*, No. 50 Church Street, New York.

The large buildings in lower Manhattan contain more than 15,000 H. P. of steam boilers equipped with the Balanced Draft System. This system automatically controls the air supplied to the furnace and limits it to practically the theoretical amount required to burn enough coal to maintain steam pressure. Any excess of air beyond this amount would dilute the gases, reduce the furnace temperature and, consequently, the efficiency of the furnace and boiler.

In order to attain this limiting of the air supply, the draft is "balanced" and atmospheric pressure is maintained in the furnace chamber at the fire door. So long as this condition is maintained, only enough air to support combustion passes through the bed of fuel and no excess is drawn in through the open door

or through cracks and crevices in the brick work above the grate. This balance is automatically maintained for all rates of combustion and all conditions of the fire.

The Balanced Draft System reduces the fuel bills, by limiting the amount of coal burned to the minimum necessary to keep up the boiler pressure, irrespective of the amount that is fed into the furnace.

In the combustion of fuel in a steam-boiler furnace two elements are to be considered: the fuel and the air. The latter is supplied by either natural or artificial draft and is either drawn or forced through the furnace. In the ordinary boiler furnace, the lack of correspondence between the air supplied and the varying load on the boiler causes much waste of coal, even with mechanical stokers or good hand firing. Every pound of coal burned on the grate needs just so much air to make it give the maximum intensity of heat. Under ordinary conditions the air supplied is controlled by regulating either the suction of the chimney or the pressure of the forced draft. With Balanced Draft, both the air supplied to the

THE EAST RIVER AND THE BROOKLYN BRIDGES FROM THE SINGER TOWER

furnace and the exhaust of gases from the furnace are under perfect control and bear a fixed relation to each other for all rates of combustion. Balanced Draft, therefore, checks the waste of coal by automatically varying both the air supply to the furnace and the throttling of the gases passing to the chimney, thereby controlling the combustion according to the evaporation, and maintaining it at its maximum efficiency under all conditions of load on the boiler.

That the Balanced-Draft System plays a very important part in the economy of the boiler plant in the Singer Building is very clearly shown by the results of the official tests, which indicate the evaporation from and at 212° F. of 10.3 pounds of water per pound of No. 2 buckwheat coal costing $2.75 per ton delivered.

It is interesting to note that this plant develops a kilowatt hour from three pounds of No. 2 buckwheat coal at a cost of $\frac{3.6}{100}$ of a cent. These results clearly demonstrate the plant in the Singer Building to be one of the most economical in the country and to compare very favorably with the great electric-power generating plants. The effect of limiting the air supply by the Balanced-Draft System is clearly shown by the CO_2 recorder, which shows an average of 16 per cent. CO_2 in the flue gases while the foregoing results are being obtained.

SMOKE BREECHING AND DUCT FOR BALANCED DRAFT

THE smoke breeching for the battery of five boilers, aggregating about 2,000 nominal H.P., consists of No. 10 gauge black iron stiffened with 2½-inch angle irons placed 3 feet on centers. There are several clean-out doors and a main damper on roller bearings. On account of its great size it was made of two sheets of steel riveted together with channel braces.

The breeching is 4 ft. x 6 ft. 6 in. at the extreme end and increases gradually to 6 ft. 6 in. x 9 ft. where it enters the vertical smoke stack. It is covered throughout its entire length with 2 inch 85 per cent. carbonate of magnesia blocks, on a wire lath foundation, leaving an air space of 1 inch between the covering and the flue. The outside is finished with magnesia plaster having a hard, smooth finish.

The entire equipment was installed by *Edwin Burhorn*, No. 71 Wall Street, who also furnished the galvanized-iron duct work connecting the balanced-draft blower with the ashpits of the boilers. This work is constructed of galvanized iron up to the rear wall and of hard-burned salt-glazed tile pipe under each boiler. To install it so as not to interfere with the concrete foundations required considerable ingenuity.

[90]

VACUUM CLEANER SYSTEM

NOT least among the mechanical features which have been introduced into the Singer Building is the Vacuum Cleaner System, which is one of the largest that has been installed in New York City.

This equipment is a special feature in the Singer Building. It is not only designed to take care of the regular cleaning of the halls, offices, walls, rugs, etc., but a special Vacuum Cleaner is installed in each office, or suite of offices, for the use of tenants. The vacuum is maintained on this special system at all hours of the usual office day and can be used by the tenant at his convenience.

The vacuum pumps used with this system, constituting a very important part of it, are arranged in three units, there being two **VACUUM PUMPS** large units, each having capacity to operate twelve to fifteen sweepers, and one small unit with a capacity to operate four to eight sweepers. These pumps are of the horizontal steam-driven pattern, and are fitted with Cincinnati Gear Air Cylinders.

The governor used with the pumps is especially designed for this class of work and is a combination speed and vacuum governor, the speed feature of which is very similar to the usual engine governor; it is a limiting device which controls the speed of the pump. The vacuum part of the governor is arranged so that it can be set for any desired vacuum, and in action will reduce the speed from the maximum maintained by the speed governor to whatever lower limit of speed is necessary to prevent the vacuum exceeding the limit for which governors are set. Thus the action of the complete governor maintains a uniform vacuum up to the limit of the capacity of the pump. Under this arrangement excessive vacuum is entirely avoided and the pumps are operated only to the extent required, so as to secure the utmost economy in consumption of steam.

The system of dust separation is what is known as "double separation," being a combination of dry **DUST SEPARATION** and wet separators. It consists of two large galvanized iron tanks, the first of which receives the dust-laden air from the building, and by a combination of centrifugal action and gravitation precipitates all the dust from the air, excepting that which is so light as to follow the air currents.

From the dry separator the air containing the light dust is discharged into the wet separators below the water line, and there, by special means, is broken up into very small particles and forced through the water in such a manner as to eliminate every particle of dust, and allow the air, free from dust, to pass to and through the cylinders of the pumps, and from there to the outer atmosphere.

The system of vacuum pipes in the Singer Building is naturally very elaborate and extensive and consists of a series of mains in the sub-**VACUUM PIPES** cellar, from which a number of risers are taken off and extended up through the building, some of them to the top of the Tower.

The risers for the special service in the offices are kept separate from the risers for general cleansing, though all are connected to the same system of horizontal pipes already referred to. Outlets are placed in the various risers in each story, to which are attached special fittings arranged for connection of the vacuum hose.

The arrangement of hose, renovators, etc., in this building is not materially different from any other vacuum cleaner system.

The special service for the use of tenants consists of $\frac{1}{2}$-inch outlets arranged under each lavatory **SPECIAL SERVICE FOR TENANTS** throughout the building, of which there are nearly four hundred, to which is permanently attached a short length of $\frac{1}{2}$-inch hose. This hose is arranged to coil up and be supported on special hooks under the lavatory, and attached to its end is a specially designed renovator for cleaning hats, clothing, etc.

The vacuum is on this system at all times, right up to the renovator itself. To avoid the intake of air, with its corresponding noise, which would exist if these renovators were not closed off when out of use, they are fitted with an automatic closing valve, which is easily operated by the thumb, and is held open during the entire period of use. The release of the renovator causes the closing of the valve.

These hat and coat renovators were designed and first used in this building, and as a matter of fact have not been used in any other building up to this time.

This special vacuum system for the convenience and comfort of the tenants, places this building in a somewhat higher position from the rental standpoint than other office buildings not so equipped.

The installation of the entire Vacuum Cleaner System was placed in the hands of the *Vacuum Cleaner Company*, with general offices at No. 425 Fifth Avenue, New York, and factories at Plainfield, N. J.

HOT WATER FOR DOMESTIC PURPOSES

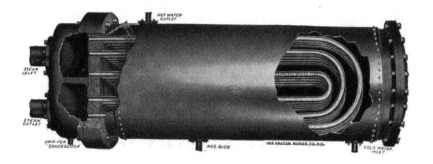

ALL of the hot water used in the Singer Building for domestic purposes, through 2,500 hot-water faucets and 125 slop sinks, is supplied by two Patterson Hot-Water Service Heaters, manufactured by *Frank L. Patterson & Co.*, No. 26 Cortlandt Street, New York. Works at Passaic, N. J.

These heaters are of the horizontal type, as shown in the accompanying illustration, and are suspended from the ceiling of the compressor room. The shells of these heaters are of boiler plate. The tube heads and exhaust steam chambers are of cast iron, as are also the removable heads. The tubes are of "U" shaped seamless drawn brass, a form that provides for the free contraction and expansion of every individual tube. Each end is secured in the heavy tube head by means of a roller expander.

In operation, the cold water enters the bottom of the shell near one end and, after being heated to a temperature of 180° F., leaves the top at the other end. There is ample storage capacity, so that a sudden demand is provided for at all times.

The largest heater is 32 inches in diameter and 128 inches long. It has a storage capacity of 280 gallons and contains 100 square feet of tubes 1¼ inch in diameter. This heater is built for a pressure of 150 pounds per square inch and supplies all of the hot water used in the building exclusive of the Tower. The smaller heater is 28 inches in diameter and 108

inches long. It contains 75 square feet of tubes 1¼ inch in diameter and has a storage capacity of 160 gallons. This heater is built for a pressure of 500 pounds per square inch and furnishes all of the hot water used in the halls and rooms of the Tower.

The pipe connections of both heaters are as follows:

The inlets for the cold water and the outlets for the hot water are 2½ inches and the steam inlets and outlets are 4 inches in diameter. The outlets for the condensed steam are 1¼ inch and the blow-off connections are also 1¼ inch in diameter.

A particularly valuable feature in connection with the heaters is the removable heads, which are far superior to the usual manhole, because the opening is equal to the full diameter of the shell and gives free access to the interior without disconnecting any pipes.

Another distinctive feature lies in the Patterson method of supporting the horizontal tubes. A perforated semi-disk of lead, drilled to match the lower half of the tube head, is placed near the free end of the tubes. The lower half of each "U" shaped tube passes through it and may move freely, as required by its contraction and expansion, without damage to itself. The lead, being softer, receives the wear that would come on the thin brass tubes if the usual iron frame were used.

FEED-WATER HEATER

THE Linton Combination Feed-Water Heater, Purifier, Oil Separator, Muffler, Return Tank and Pump Governor, installed in the Singer Building, performs all the functions indicated by its title.

It is primarily an "open" feed-water heater, is of the horizontal type and is 72 inches in diameter and 144 inches long. The exhaust steam inlet and outlet connections are 20 inches in diameter. This Combination contains some new and improved features, especial attention being given to the satisfactory separation of the oil from the exhaust steam and for accessibility to the interior. The exhaust steam upon entering is introduced into the large expansion chamber where its velocity is greatly retarded, from there it passes through a perforated baffle plate where it is broken up, and thence through separating screens. These screens are of $\frac{1}{4}$-inch wire mesh and thoroughly remove all oil in the exhaust allowing it to be used in the heating system of the building and the returns from same to be taken back to the heater and from there into the boilers. The oil is drained off to be re-used and the steam passes

on, over and around the heating trays where it mingles with the feed water, heating it to its temperature, 212° F. A perfectly tight diaphragm prevents the liberated oil from coming in contact with the feed water. The entire heads of the Combination are removable without disturbing any connections, which allows the whole interior to be readily examined and the trays, filter box and screens to be easily removed, making it the most accessible of any heater manufactured.

As the returns from the heating system of the building form a considerable part of the feed water but little fresh cold water is introduced. The feed water passes from tray to tray in opposite directions and from there into the filter box where it is filtered through coke and looses any foreign matter that has already been deposited on the heating trays. It is then pumped to the boilers, this being automatically controlled by the pump governor, a part of the Combination, consisting of a special balanced valve operated by a copper float.

The Linton Combination is manufactured by the *Linton Machine Company*, No. 26 Cortlandt Street, New York City.

INSULATION

ONE of the many and varied problems in connection with the mechanical equipment of the Singer Building is that of Heat Insulation.

In order best to conserve all of the immense energy, to effect and maintain the highest degree of efficiency

HEAT INSULATION commensurate with that splendid work of the craftsmen, the Power Plant, the use of the best methods and materials attainable was essential.

To the *Robert A. Keasbey Co.*, No. 100 North Moore Street, New York, was intrusted a very large part of this important detail of equipment.

One of the most interesting features of this work is the non-conducting fireproof ceiling suspended

NON-CONDUCTING CEILING over the machinery rooms, about 14 inches below and supported from the main floor structural framing by galvanized flat iron, carrying tee and angle irons so arranged that frames are formed, into which are set 85 per cent. carbonate of magnesia blocks 2 inches thick, over which is stretched 2-inch galvanized hexagon mesh wire, tightly drawn and secured. On this is applied a coat of 85 per cent. carbonate of magnesia plaster $\frac{1}{2}$ inch thick, finished with two coats of hard finishing cement.

This construction permits the circulation of air by means of blowers, completely baffling the radiation of heat, either from above or below the ceiling, and presents a uniformly good appearance.

Heated surfaces lose heat through radiation and conduction when coming into contact with a cooler

ECONOMY OF GOOD INSULATION body or element. This principle was constantly borne in mind when insulating the 14-inch main steam header, the 20-inch exhaust line, the hot- and cold-water circulating lines, feed-water heater, blow-off and drip tanks, engine cylinders, ducts and flue.

Pipes and boilers carrying steam at 212° F. and upward coming into direct contact with the surrounding atmosphere, the temperature of which seldom reaches 100° F., lose a large percentage of heat through radiation. This loss causes condensation, which must be overcome to maintain the plant's efficiency, and the only recourse is the excessive use of fuel.

A recent test shows that the saving of fuel, taking steam at 100 pounds' pressure through a bare pipe, as compared with its conveyance through a properly insulated pipe, will amount to more than $1.217 per year for each square foot of pipe; the formula of computation being as follows:

Steam at 100 pounds' pressure, bare pipe, loses per square foot, iron measure, a minute, 13 B. T. U. by covering with 85 per cent. carbonate of magnesia sections 1.196 inches thick, the loss per square foot iron measure, per minute, is 2.13 B. T. U.; therefore 13—2.13=10.87 B. T. U. saved.

Saving by the use of good insulation: 10.87 B. T. U. × 525600 minutes in a year—875 Latent Heat Units in 1 lb. of steam at 100 lbs. pressure=6530.6 lbs. of water condensed (saved)—8 lbs. of water evaporated per pound of coal=816.32 lbs. of coal saved at $3 per ton=$1.217 saved per year per square foot of iron covered.

Some idea of the saving at the Singer Plant resulting from the method used and quality of the insulation furnished may be had when one comprehends:

First, the boiler pressure is 200 pounds.

Second, there are about 75,000 square feet of steam surfaces, or about 2 acres, insulated with 85 per cent. carbonate of magnesia in scientifically determined thicknesses, ranging from $\frac{1}{2}$ inch to 4 inches.

In this manner the heat in the lines is confined, preventing its loss through radiation, conduction or condensation.

Fuel is the most expensive item of cost in the operation of a power plant, and the saving of fuel is an important factor in the earnings of any plant, large or small, tremendously so in the Power Plant designed to equip the Singer Building.

Concerning the 9,000 square feet exposed surfaces of brine, ammonia and ice-water lines in

COLD INSULATION connection with the compression machine, one need only realize that the 1$\frac{1}{2}$-inch ice-water lines in basement discharge water at 38°, at the extreme top of Tower, 612 feet above street level, with outlets in almost every room.

Cooled surfaces, i. e., brine and ammonia lines lose efficiency through absorption when coming into contact with a warmer body or element.

Cork, by nature, contains an infinite number of

CORK AS A NON-CONDUCTOR entrapped air cells, rendering it an excellent non-conductor of heat and cold, is very light in weight and will not absorb moisture, hence its use.

STEAM ENGINES

THE prime movers in the Power Plant of the Singer Building consist of five Ball & Wood Corliss Valve, Non-Releasing Gear Engines of the following types and normal ratings: Two Cross Compounds having high-pressure cylinders, 17 inches diameter, low-pressure cylinders 29 inches diameter, length of stroke 27 inches; two Simples, each having cylinders 21 inches diameter, 27 inches length of stroke, all of 480 H.P. each; and one Simple, having cylinder 17 inches diameter, length of stroke 27 inches, and rated 320 H.P.

Each engine operates at a speed of 150 revolutions per minute at 150 pounds' steam pressure with free atmospheric exhaust and is directly connected to a direct current Diehl Generator.

The *Ball & Wood Company* is the originator and builder of the first successful Non-releasing Gear, Corliss Valve Engine, and during the past fifteen years has installed many in some of the most prominent power plants in the country.

The aim of the originator was to realize all of the advantages of the Corliss Valve and to eliminate the disadvantages resulting from the releasing gear. The steam economies realized, as well as the well-proved ability to carry not only loads at ratings but heavy overloads, justify the Company's plan. The admission valves of the high- and low-pressure cylinders are controlled by the Ball & Wood Governor, while the exhaust valves are actuated through independent eccentrics. Wide range of cut-off is thus obtained and great flexibility in adjustment permissible. Not only is the steam economy of the best, but the floor space required per horse-power very much less than that demanded by the releasing gear types. At the same time a higher mechanical efficiency results.

Under variable load conditions the mean economy shows the advantage of the Ball & Wood System.

An important feature of any power plant, especially when high pressures are carried, is the steam piping. The best types of engines and boilers may be installed and the plant fail because of unreliable piping. The *Ball & Wood Company*, believing, as it does, in the best methods, recognized the weakness in any system in which joints could leak, even in cases of installations in which it was the purpose and plan of the engineers and purchasers to apply the best methods, and to this end developed what is now well known as the Ball-Wood Welded Flanged Pipe and Bends. The boilers of the Singer Building Power Plant are fitted with the Ball-Wood Welded Flanged Pipe and Pipe Bends.

VALVE INSTALLATION

PILOT VALVE

EACH of the five boilers (four 400 H.P. and one 320 H.P.) in the Singer Building are fitted with the *Foster Engineering Company's* Combination, Automatic Non-Return and Emergency Stop Valves. (See illustration.)

These valves are used for preventing a back-flow of steam into a broken or defective boiler in the event

PILOT OR STEAM-GOV-ERNING VALVES of the blowing out of a tube, poor firing, a drop in pressure, etc., the valves automatically closing if the header pressure exceeds the boiler pressure slightly, remaining open when the pressure of the five boilers is equalized. In addition, they also automatically close, cutting off the entire battery of five boilers should the header or any of the steam lines break, or in the event of a rupture, etc.

On the face of each boiler, mounted on the polished brick surface, is located the Pilot or Governing Valve; the diaphragm chamber of this valve is connected by a system of extra heavy brass auxiliary piping (concealed within the wall) to the header and the main steam line. There are two connections to this Pilot Valve: one on the inlet side takes steam from the boiler direct and remains closed under normal conditions. The outlet or discharge side of this Pilot Valve is connected to the closing piston of the main boiler valve.

In the event of a rupture, as above referred to,

the pressure in the diaphragm chamber drops, opening the Pilot Valve and allowing the steam from the boiler to pass through it to the closing piston, thus closing the valves automatically.

This Pilot or Governing Valve is highly polished and finished and presents an attractive appearance. On the inlet connection, just within the union, is located a small strainer, which serves to prevent the passage of foreign matter that may be carried through the pipe, thus preventing the Governing Valve from leaking.

Each Pilot Valve is equipped with two gauges, finished and polished, one indicating the boiler pressure and the other the line pressure, so that at a glance the engineers can note the pressure on their lines at all times.

At a point some 250 feet distant from the boiler room, in the Chief Engineer's office, there are located

EMERGENCY VALVES on the wall and mounted on an elaborately finished marble gauge board of unique design, five emergency valves (one for each boiler).

These emergency valves are simply ¾-inch brass-finished globe valves, each equipped with a polished gauge that records the main steam-line pressure. By their use the Chief Engineer, without leaving his chair, can by the mere cracking of one of these valves cut out or control any one or all of the boilers in the battery at will.

These valves are likewise connected with the Pilot or Governing Valve in the boiler room by the brass auxiliary piping carried through the building and concealed within the walls.

Opening one of the Emergency Valves bleeds the steam from the diaphragm chamber of the distant Pilot or Governing Valve, having the same effect on the main valve as a break in the line, be-

EMERGENCY VALVE

cause it then admits boiler pressure through the Pilot to its closing piston, thus automatically bringing the main boiler valve to its seat as previously explained.

This emergency feature is particularly valuable to the Chief Engineer, as it not only permits him to control any boiler at will without the necessity of operating the hand wheel of the main valve on the top of the boiler, but it also provides means for closing off the entire battery in case of emergency.

The small quantity of steam that is bled through these emergency valves when used as described is conveyed to a brass manifold, highly polished, immediately beneath the gauge board, and from thence is carried off beneath the floors. The whole arrangement is neat and compact and presents a very pleasing appearance as one enters the Chief Engineer's office. It not only insures automatic control of each or all of the boilers, but also manual control without the necessity of access to the top of the boilers.

DIVISION VALVE

On the 12-inch main steam lines, midway on each side, are located two 12-inch Foster Special Division Valves, steam actuated.

SPECIAL DIVI-SION VALVES In the event of a rupture in any of the steam lines, and after the automatic cutting out of the boilers, as previously described, the broken section of the main line can be isolated by the opening of a fourway cock, controlled by a chain (by which steam is admitted to the closing piston), closing off these Division Valves and permitting steam to be thrown on the opposite side of the header and the building, thus allowing the operation of the various units not affected by the rupture, without hindrance or without loss of service during the time required to make repairs to the broken side.

These valves are especially efficient in that they insure against the complete closing for any length of time of the entire plant in the event of an accident to either side of the header. They are heavy and substantial looking and sensitive in their operation.

On the Balanced Draft Equipment to the boilers, controlling the engine feeding the blower, is connected a Foster Automatic Fan Engine Regulating Valve, operating within a variation of a pound and a half. A drop in the boiler pres-

FAN ENGINE REGULATING VALVE sure automatically opens this valve, feeds steam to the engine and accelerates the speed of the blower. When steam reaches the adjusted boiler pressure, the valve automatically stops the fan engine. It is likewise provided with a limit screw for controlling

the speed of the fan engine and has a by-pass arrangement by which the engine can be kept creeping without load when the boiler pressure is at its normal height.

On the heating system the *Foster Engineering Company's* special regulating valve is installed, re-

SPECIAL VALVES FOR HEATING SYSTEM ducing boiler pressure to the required heating pressure for the building.

On the 20-inch automatic exhaust line from the heating lines is mounted a 20-inch Foster Back-Pressure Valve, of unique design and construction, without outside dash pots, levers, or weights, maintaining a constant back pressure on the heating system and automatically opening to the atmosphere when steam is reached beyond the adjusted amount.

The high- and low-duty water pumps are fitted with a Foster Special Class G Auxiliary Operated

PUMP GOVERN-ING VALVES Pump Governor (see illustration), for controlling the water discharge, maintaining a constant pressure and preventing the pump from racing. These governors work within a very close regulation and are of an attractive design. They are all composition, fitted with small phosphor bronze diaphragms.

The plant is also fitted with Foster regulating and reducing valves on the line to the hot-water tanks,

MISCELLANE-OUS VALVES on the heating line to the oil tanks, and on the air line to the sterilizers of the barber shop and chiropodist and manicuring parlors. These valves are all of the Special Class G construction, single seated, auxiliary operated, regulating within a close degree; a special valve of a similar construction is likewise placed on the air lines operating the handsomely finished bronze gates of each elevator on each floor, reducing 100 pounds to 50 pounds air required to control these gates. All the devices of the *Foster Engineering Company* are of the latest design and construction and are especially adapted to the work for which they are intended.

PUMP GOVERNOR

To those interested in the problem of reducing and regulating steam or air for work of this nature, the Foster installation in the Singer Building is well worthy a visit, and to a practical engineer, who is thrown in contact with devices of this nature, they furnish an interesting study.

STEAM SEPARATORS

ENGINE No. 4.—SHOWING COCHRANE VERTICAL STEAM SEPARATOR

THE engines are located in a separate room, some distance from the boilers, so that the steam must pass through a considerable length of piping before it reaches the engines.

To protect the engines from water which might be condensed from the steam in the pipes, and also from water due to priming or foaming of the boilers, or possibly to a too high water level, Cochrane Steam Separators, manufactured by the *Harrison Safety Boiler Works* of Philadelphia, Pa., were placed in the steam lines, close to the engines and pumps. A Cochrane Separator consists essentially of a closed vessel in which a ribbed baffle plate is placed directly in front of the current of steam. In this way, any particles of moisture are projected against the baffle plate, whence they flow into a well or receiver, drained by an automatic steam trap. The steam passes around the sides of the baffle and enters the engine in a dry condition.

These separators not only protect engines by keeping out large masses of water which might cause disruption of cylinders but, by stopping small amounts of moisture which are always found in steam and which are increased by condensation in the steam main, they prevent the washing away of cylinder lubricating oil, thereby reducing the expense of oil and minimizing friction and wear.

There are six Cochrane Separators in the Singer Building Power Plant, one of the horizontal type and the remainder of the vertical receiver type.

The receiver type is so called because it is supplied with a very large well or receiver, which serves not only to hold large volumes of water until they can be drained out by the trap, but also equalizes the flow of steam and maintains a more uniform pressure at the engines. This volume of steam in the receiver also acts as a cushion to absorb the pulsations of the column of steam in the pipe line.

REFRIGERATING PLANT

THE cooling of the drinking water used throughout the Singer Building is produced by means of the most modern and up-to-date refrigerating machinery.

The water used in the drinking-water system is first put through a battery of water filters, after which it is forced into the cooling tanks.

These tanks are two in number, one for high-pressure service and one for low pressure. Each tank is 42 inches in diameter and 10 feet long, and is provided with approximately 1,025 feet of 1¼-inch extra heavy continuous welded pipe coils. These coils are arranged with all the necessary headers, valves, fittings and connections for the circulation of cold brine. From this combined cooling and supply tank, the water is circulated throughout the entire building and Tower by means of two stage turbine pumps, these pumps being directly connected to motors. There are three of these pumps, each having a capacity of 50 gallons per minute; two of the pumps are designed for a working pressure of 300 pounds per square inch, and one for 100 pounds per square inch. The refrigerating machine of this plant is provided with two vertical single-acting compressors, driven by a Corliss-Valve Engine. This machine, as well as the balance of the refrigerating machinery throughout the plant, was built and installed by the *York Manufacturing Company*, of York, Pa. For cooling the brine circulated in the water-cooling coils two double-pipe brine coolers are used, each cooler being 12 pipes high and 18 feet 2 inches long of 2-inch and 3-inch pipe. The brine is taken from a brine supply tank and circulated through the brine coolers and water-cooling coils by means of a duplex direct-acting pump.

In connection with this water-cooling system a small freezing system is installed, which produces from 500 to 1,000 pounds of ice per day. This system has proved very satisfactory, and gives a continuous supply of cold drinking water throughout the building at all times.

ELECTRICAL INSTALLATION

MANY novel and serious problems were presented by the plans devised for the electric lighting and the furnishing of power for the Singer Building, but these were all satisfactorily solved, and each electric system installed is in every respect complete and adequate to meet every demand upon it.

The electric generators and motors used in the **ELECTRIC GENERATING APPARATUS** Singer Building were made by the *Diehl Manufacturing Company* of Elizabethport, N. J., and were selected because of confidence in their reliability and economy, as shown by their successful operation in many varieties of service.

The dynamos are compound wound multipolar slow-speed engine type generators, four machines having a capacity of 300 K.W. each and one of 200 K.W., all supplying current at 250 volts at 150 R.P.M. They furnish the entire supply of electric current used throughout the building for both lighting and power.

These generators are of massive design, with low heat limits due to low current density in windings, commutator and brushes and to excellent ventilation afforded by paths for air currents through all of the windings and interior parts of the machines. They are non-sparking at all loads and are capable of standing heavy overloads for long periods of time.

During the building construction they successfully stood continuous overloads of from 50 to 75 per cent. without sparking or injurious heating, conditions being especially unfavorable, due to the unavoidable presence of dust and dirt incident to the building operations.

Electric power has proved a vital factor in the development of the modern office building. Many **ELECTRIC MOTORS** problems where power is required would be difficult if not impossible of solution were it not for the adaptability and flexibility of the electric motor.

When office buildings were moderate in size the number of persons occupying them was comparatively small. Under such conditions natural means could be depended upon to provide ventilation which, while by no means adequate, was the best that could be obtained. With development and gradual increase in size, problems were introduced on the solution of which depended the success or failure of the building. The mammoth structures of the present day accommodate many thousands of persons, making the question of ventilation of supreme importance. Many cases arise in planning for ventilation where natural means are inadequate and mechanical means must be provided. Proper machinery must be placed in situations that are inaccessible and remote from the source of power. The electrically driven fan or blower is perfectly adapted to such conditions because it can be placed in any position without regard to other apparatus.

Other problems arise, the great importance of

which are not apparent to the uninitiated observer, which have to do with auxiliaries in the power plant. The engine room may be said to be the heart of the building, for the reason that the power plant supplies the building with light and heat as well as power. The space allowed is necessarily small, while apparatus for many different purposes are required. The electric motor again proves its value here, being used to drive pumps of different kinds as well as special machinery incident to the operation of the building.

It will be noted that the service required of electric motors in the modern office building is exacting, and they must be thoroughly reliable and well adapted to the work they are to perform. They are frequently called upon to run, fully loaded, continuously for many hours, and failure would interfere seriously with the successful operation of the building.

The *Diehl Manufacturing Company* makes a specialty of motors for the purposes outlined, and the motors installed in the Singer Building are noteworthy for their efficient, sparkless running and low heat limits. The motors are strongly and compactly built and all parts subject to wear have generous allowance to insure great durability.

The motors drive ventilating fans located in various parts of the building, from the 39th floor to the engine room in the basement. They are also used to drive pumps for ice-water circulation through the building and for emptying the drain pit in the basement into the sewer. The Vacuum Cleaner

System is driven by a motor and the liquid in the brine tanks is agitated by similar means. Other uses of the motors are conventional application for ordinary power purposes.

The system of electrical distribution was furnished and installed by the *M. B. Foster Electric Company*, having its principal office

ELECTRICAL DISTRIBUTION at No. 109 West Twenty-sixth Street, New York City, and a branch office at No. 220 Devonshire Street, Boston. Edward S. Clinch, Jr., is the President of the Company, and Mortimer B. Foster, Secretary and Treasurer.

The installation includes the electric light and power, wiring, generator leads, switch board, panel boards, telephone conduits, watchman's time detector and a low-tension system for supplying current for operating bells and similar apparatus.

The switchboard was built by the *Diehl Manufacturing Company* of Elizabethport, N. J. The slabs

SWITCH BOARD are of white Italian marble and have a copper-plated bronze base. The switch board is of the most approved style. There is not a fuse on it. The generators and feeders are protected by the I.T.E. circuit breakers of the double-pole double-arm laminated type, and the circuit breakers protecting the generators have the reverse current-release attachment. The office of this attachment is to prevent the demagnetizing or reversing of the generators. The indicating instruments are of the illuminating dial type, manufactured by the *Weston Electrical Instrument Company* of Newark. The weight of the switch board as it stands, excepting the indicating instruments and watt-meters, is 17,100 pounds, of which 8,400 pounds are copper, 5,400 pounds marble and 3,300 pounds iron.

Although the 220 volt, 2-wire system is used for both lighting and power, the lighting feeders are of

WIRING SYSTEM the 3-wire double neutral loop system, so arranged that it may readily be changed from the 3 to the 2-wire system. It also maintains an absolutely even voltage on every floor no matter at what distance from the switch board.

The generator leads are paper insulated lead-covered cables, and contain 6,185 pounds of copper. All the feeders and branch wires, from the basement to the top of the Tower, are rubber covered, of the "Tip Top" brand, and have an aggregate length of 67 miles, including 1,699,714 feet of single wire, and 53,950 pounds of copper. This amount of copper will make sufficient No. 14 wire, which is the size used for branch work, to reach from New York to Chicago.

The largest feeder ever run to a similar height is that which runs to the 36th floor, feeding the elevators in the Tower. This feeder weighs 9,710 pounds and each conductor is 670 feet long.

The wire and generator leads were manufactured by the *Standard Underground Cable Company* of Pittsburg. The current carried by each feeder is measured by an integrating wattmeter, made by the *Sangamo Electric Company*.

All wires are run in electro-duct iron conduit, made by the *American Circular Loom Company* of Chelsea, Mass. The conduit used weighs 105 tons, and has an aggregate length of 30 miles, or over twice the distance from the Battery to Spuyten Duyvil.

The panel boards are of marbleized slate with the main and each branch circuit protected by

PANEL BOARDS National Electric Code enclosed fuses. A unique idea was carried out on these panels in covering the bus bars and cross connection bars with fiber. This is the first time this has ever been done, although it reduces to a minimum the possibility of anyone causing a short circuit by accidentally placing a tool or other conductor across the bus bars.

Very few brackets have been used in the building. The general lighting of the offices is by means of ceiling clusters, and receptacles are installed in the baseboard for desk lights.

CEILING LIGHTS There are 1,342 ceiling outlets, 441 bracket outlets, 1,902 base receptacles, with a capacity of 7,612 16-candle power lights, and 989 flush push switches.

The main corridor of the building is one of the most artistic and beautiful of any building in the city, and a system of lighting was absolutely necessary that would not in any respect detract from the artistic qualities of the corridor. The principal light is derived from clusters of 48 8-candle power lamps placed in the top of each dome in the ceiling and above amber rippled glass. In addition to these ceiling clusters, there are bronze brackets with ground glass globes. The general effect produced

VIEW OF MAIN CORRIDOR LOOKING EAST, SHOWING CEILING LIGHTS
(See description on preceding page)

s an illumination with no shadows, which gives a daylight effect to the whole corridor and thereby displays all its artistic features and yet is so soft and diffusive as not in any degree to make its presence unpleasantly evident.

The greatest and most noteworthy innovation in the whole electric equip-

EXTERIOR LIGHTING ment of the Singer Building is the illumination of the exterior of the Tower at night. Never before has any building been thus illuminated, the idea being conceived by Charles G. Armstrong, Consulting Mechanical and Electrical Engineer of the building. This illumination is accomplished by thirty 18-inch projectors, designed expressly for the purpose by the General Electric Company of Schenectady. The beams of light from the projectors are thrown upon the exterior walls of the Tower from its base to the 35th floor, and the remainder of the exterior is illuminated by 1,600 concealed incandescent lamps.

The flag on the flag pole of the Tower is illuminated by the projection of a beam of light from a 36-inch projector on the roof of the Bourne Building, and the name "SINGER" can, therefore, wave in the breeze both day and night before the eyes of the public.

ELECTRICAL MEASURING INSTRUMENTS

INDICATING Electrical Measuring Instruments are of even more importance to the electrical engineer than is the action of the human pulse to a physician, and upon the use of such devices entirely depends the knowledge of an electrical plant's action.

To avoid danger, the Voltmeter must always be relied upon for throwing two generating sets in parallel, and it is the only guide the operator has for maintaining a steady light throughout the entire building. This instrument is always referred to for determining whether the electric lights are burning at their rated efficiency, and shows the direct relation of coal bills to renewal of lamps.

The Ammeter has a very important duty in detecting the amount of current (or "load") on any generating set or distributing device, so that it may be known whether each is doing its share of the work and not becoming strained or damaged by "overload." This type of meter also facilitates an economical control of feeder circuits by indicating to the operator the branches of the building that are unnecessarily taking current.

Of course when the functions of these instruments are thoroughly understood to be so essential to the successful, economical and uninterrupted operation of the plant, an engineer will select the very best apparatus the market affords. The choice of *Weston Electrical Measuring Instruments* has given the Singer Building the benefit of the world's highest achievement in the art of electrical measurement, and allows the engineer of that plant to know at all times within 1 per cent. of the actual instantaneous values of voltage and amperage that obtain.

RUBBER PRODUCTS

RUBBER, too, has played its part in the construction and equipment of this edifice. It has furnished its invaluable assistance in many ways.

Without rubber suction hose and rubber steam hose, the excavations for the foundations would have been practically impossible. Rubber discharge hose has been necessary to convey water from one point to another. None of the pneumatic hammers, thousands of which were daily employed in riveting the vast structure together, could have been nearly so promptly and efficiently handled without rubber pneumatic hose.

Many people do not know that the best rubber is grown directly under the equator, where the fierce beams of the tropical sun develop the caoutchouc or rubber tree. The torrential rains of the wet season in the tropics have also much to do with fostering its growth and development.

The crude sap is gathered by puncturing the tree at intervals around its greatest girth and collecting the sap, as it exudes, in little cups. Afterwards this is hardened by being smoked over a fire of nut indigenous to the same soil. This nut will not flame or blaze when lighted, but produces a thick and heavy smoke, which when brought into contact with the rubber milk coagulates it and renders it fit for transportation.

As one departs from the equator, rubber still grows, but the qualities are poorer and poorer, until they are nearly resins.

The use of this commodity is so extended that, independent of the purely mechanical devices in which it forms a part, goods of an ornamental and elegant nature, too, are made from it.

Among its latest developments is a rubber floor covering, or tile, made up as burned china tiling is made, of a number of different colored pieces, of different shapes, to represent any design. This forms a most beautiful floor covering—durable, sanitary, non-slippery, and much more desirable for the purpose than anything yet devised.

The elevator cars in the Singer Building are furnished with it, from designs supplied by the *Gutta Percha & Rubber Manufacturing Co.* of No. 126 Duane Street, New York, who also supplied the other rubber material used in the construction and equipment of this building.

OIL FILTRATION

THE Multiplex Type "White Star" Oil Filter installed in the Singer Building by the *Van Dyck Churchill Co.*, engineers and contractors of Continuous Oiling System, 91 and 93 Liberty Street, New York, is designed to meet the demand in large power stations for great capacity in limited area, and is claimed to be the only apparatus that can perfectly purify lubricating oil in quantity.

In the early days of the manufacture and installation of the "White Star" Continuous Oiling System, difficulty was occasionally experienced in the handling of thickened or emulsified oils. Emulsion of the lubricating oils used in a power plant is of common occurrence and the makers of this filter attacked this problem with the determination to solve it if possible. After much experimenting that was costly in time and money, a successful method of treatment was devised.

It is an undisputed fact that the only simple, scientific and absolutely effectual method for the thorough purification of lubricating oils is employed in the "White Star" Oil Filter, and in such a compact form that no other device of the kind can approach its remarkable capacity in an equal area.

In this type the separating chamber is entirely independent of the storage chambers, the communicating pipes being controlled from the outside.

In the storage chambers, numbers of filtering cylinders are suspended in such a manner that they may be detached individually for cleaning without interrupting the operation of the others.

Multiplex filters are formed around angle iron framework, the bodies being made of heavy galvanized iron, with all seams riveted and caulked.

Obviously, the important item of the complete system is the Filter, whose action must be reliable and efficient at all times. Its failure to purify the oil perfectly would practically nullify the good results of the continuous lubrication, flooding the bearings with dirty oil, increasing the friction and wear and allowing the piping to fill with sediment and the oil feeds to clog.

Consequently, the "White Star" Oil Filter is an essential component of the Continuous Oiling System, to which very properly it lends its name. Perfect and continuous in its operation, easily and quickly cleaned, and ample in filtering capacity, the "White Star" Oil Filter is particularly well adapted to continuous oiling service.

OILING SYSTEM

ADMIRALTY OILING TABLE

THE Oiling System comprises two 200-gallon capacity storage tanks, one for machine and the other for cylinder oil; an oiling table of the Siegrist "Admiralty" type, having four duplex steam pumps, two for circulating the machine oil and the two others for the cylinder oil; pressure machine-oil cups on all the engines, pumps, compressors, ice machine and motors requiring lubrication; duplex vertical oil pumps on all the cylinders of the engines, pumps, etc., provided with ratchet drives connected to some reciprocating part of the engines, etc., and so arranged that they will force the cylinder oil into the engine cylinders against 175 pounds steam pressure; oil sump tank of 90 gallons capacity, to catch the machine oil drips from the engines, etc., and two machine-oil filters, of 200 gallons capacity per twenty-four hours. One of these is of Turner make.

The system is operated under a pressure of from 10 to 15 pounds per square inch, and its various appurtenances are connected together by means of brass piping.

Just as in the human body the heart pumps the blood through the various parts and organs back to the lungs, where it is purified and then recirculated, so here the Oiling System pumps the oil to the various engines, etc., from which it flows back to the sump and filter, to be cleaned and recirculated. Even the oil in the exhaust steam and drips, which is usually wasted, is here extracted, filtered, and re-used, through an appliance described in detail on another page.

LUBRICATING OILS

THE *Stephens & Conrow Co.*, of No. 136 Liberty Street, New York, who furnished the lubricating oils for the mechanical plant of the Singer Building, write as follows:

"It is with mingled pleasure and pride we sign ourselves participants in the successful operation of the motive system of the giant Singer Building, if this service is only to eliminate the friction from the working, wearing parts of the mighty valves of its complex heart. For here was set our task.

"Go down with us into the peerless Power Plant—the life center of the building, and note the perpetual activity of the numerous but interdependent mechanisms, forming with almost physiological arrangement the organism which alone makes practical the towering shaft of business homes above.

"In this domain of the engineer, our lubricating specialties, impelled by a perfect oiling system, make their ceaseless round, directly or indirectly facilitating the working of five Babcock & Wilcox boilers with superheaters; five main four-valve Ball & Wood engines, two cross compound d.c. to Diehl 300 K.W. Generators, and three d.c., one to a 200 K.W., and the two others to 300 K.W. Generators, supplying heat and power; eight auxiliary engines variously used; thirty-five pumps for boiler feeding, vacuum cleaning, water supply, etc.; sixteen Otis Traction Passenger Elevators and three plunger hydraulic freight elevators; a distilled water condenser, and a 20-ton York Ice Machine, driven by a Corliss Engine.

"A recital explaining the practical, experimental and chemical details employed in compounding oils, greases, etc., to meet the varied symptoms of this complex yet multiplex system, where no two engines, though technically identical, present the same conditions, and where the recurring disturbances of superheat, condensations, etc., have to be overcome, did space permit, would be exceedingly dry and unprofitable reading to any except ourselves. After the manner of our product, therefore, we shall have to work for the most part unseen, being content with the knowledge that we have accomplished our task."

STEAM PACKING

THE question of packing for stuffing boxes, steam joints, etc., in the mechanical plant of the Singer Building, while a small matter in itself, received the closest attention and study, always with an eye open to the fact that the packing is intended to prevent leakage of steam, and that leaks in any steam vessel bear directly on the consumption of coal and frustrate the very idea of sparing no expense in equipment to obtain economy in running. In referring to this subject, the point which naturally is uppermost in the mind of one whom the packing question interests is the piston rod and valve steam packing. These parts are packed with *Crandall's High-Pressure Ring Packing*, made up in ring form, a perfect fit to rod and stuffing box. This material is made with a large rubber core in the center to give the packing elasticity, the core being protected from the extreme heat of the stuffing box by the outside cover of the finest quality asbestos fiber, lubricated with a special compound to reduce friction. The selection of this material was apparently no mistake, as it has been found that the heavy layers of asbestos protect the rubber core, preventing deterioration and thereby prolonging the life of the packing. Other packing propositions than the above were considered and given the same close attention which has marked the successful construction of the Singer Building. To dwell on each of these propositions would be superfluous; on the high-pressure piston-rod and valve-stem work the results obtained by the use of the Crandall Packing are eminently satisfactory.

WATER FILTERS

ALL of the water used in the Singer Building for drinking and domestic purposes is purified by two Loomis-Manning Water Filters, shown in the accompanying illustration, which are manufactured by the *Loomis-Manning Filter Company*, 9203 Metropolitan Life Tower, New York. Main office and works, Philadelphia, Pa.

The water, after passing through two specially constructed horizontal filters, is refiltered and refined

by the Loomis-Manning Filters and delivered to the Water-Cooling Plant for the Drinking-Water System.

The operation of these filters is very simple, each of them being controlled by a Manning Single Multiple Valve, any function of the filter being obtained by moving the operating lever of the valve over a registered dial to any of the stations marked thereon, namely, "Filtering," "Filtering to Waste," "Washing Filter Bed," or "By-Pass."

These filters are washed by a reverse current

of water by means of the special devices composing the Loomis System of washing a filter bed.

One filter supplies the High-Service Drinking-Water System, and is built and tested out to withstand a pressure of 400 pounds. The other supplies the Low-Service Drinking-Water System and is built and tested out to withstand a pressure of 100 pounds. Each filter is composed of sections (two cylinders and two bonnets) securely bolted together, and forming as a whole a vertical cast-iron cylinder casing mounted upon a cast-iron stand.

Loomis-Manning Filters have been used in all of the Singer Buildings. In the original Singer Building a plant was installed in 1897. When the Bourne Addition was constructed a second plant was installed in 1899, and now the third plant has been installed in the completed Singer Building in 1908.

The Loomis-Manning Filters are made of both single- and double-cylinder type. The former consists of one cylinder charged with crushed flint, and fitted with an alum coagulant attachment.

In this apparatus a minute portion of alum is fed to the water as it passes into the filter. The alum coagulates the impurities in the water and deposits them in a glutinous mass on the surface of the filtering bed. When the filter is cleansed this mass is washed out into the sewer.

The double-cylinder type consists of two cylinders, one of which is charged with crushed flint quartz, while the other contains granulated bone charcoal. In this type no alum or other coagulant is required. The filtering material fills the lower half of the cylinder. The water enters at the top, passing first through the cylinder containing the quartz, which removes the impurities held in suspension; then through the charcoal cylinder, wherein all odor, taste and color are removed. It deposits all impurities on top of the filtering beds, and clear and sparkling, passes out through the pipe at the bottom of the filter.

The double-cylinder filters are more economical to operate as no alum is used, and they do not require as frequent washing as the other kind. Most of the installations made are of the double-cylinder type.

REMOVAL OF OLD AND SETTING OF NEW MECHANICAL PLANT

THE entire mechanical plant of the old building, consisting of boilers, engines, generators, pumps, tanks and various other appurtenances, was removed during the reconstruction and enlargement of the buildings and replaced by a new plant of increased capacity. This work was accomplished gradually, according to a carefully prearranged programme, as the old buildings had to be supplied uninterruptedly with water, heat and electrical current for light and power during the alterations.

Every one who has had occasion to visit the engine room of a modern building, and has wondered at the intricate arrangement of engines and piping, will readily realize what it meant to take out the old machinery and install the new without interrupting the operation of the plant.

This contract comprised the knocking down and taking out from the old plant of five Ball & Wood engines with direct-connected Diehl generators, ranging in size from 25 to 100 K.W., and weighing from 2 to 7 tons each. Also the removal of about twenty pumps and numerous tanks.

The old engines and generators were replaced by five units, four of which are of 300 K.W. capacity and one of 200 K.W. The heavier single pieces of the generators, namely, the armatures, weigh about 8 tons each, the engine frames about 8 tons, and the fly wheels, which were in halves, from 9 to 13 tons each.

This contract further included the installation of two of the largest cooling tanks ever made, one of them weighing 14 and the other 16 tons; the installation of the ice plant, weighing about 50 tons; two special fire pumps, weighing about 10 tons, and the following machine-shop tools: Two lathes, weighing about 5 tons and 2 tons, respectively; one shaper, 2 tons; one pipe-cutting machine, 2 tons; two drill presses, 3 tons; one power hacksaw, one double grinder and several smaller tools.

Throughout various floors of the building, from the basement to the 39th, several ventilating motors were installed, ranging in size from 15 to 75 H.P. This work had to be done mostly at night so as not to interfere with the street traffic and the work of construction.

The rigging used to handle the heavy parts was of sufficient strength to carry four times the load; the electrical winches used for hoisting were especially designed by the contractor for this work, *Richard Doughty*, of No. 121 Liberty Street, New York.

The execution of the contract extended over a period of one year. Notwithstanding the many difficulties encountered, the work was carried on and finished without an accident of any kind. It included not only the raising and lowering of the machinery into the building and placing it in position, but also the hauling from and to the docks.

SAFE-DEPOSIT VAULTS

MAIN CORRIDOR AND ELEVATOR
THE SAFE DEPOSIT COMPANY OF NEW YORK

ABOUT 10,000 square feet of the basement of the Singer Building is specially designed and constructed for the use of *The Safe Deposit Company of New York*, which offers its patrons the most secure, elaborate and convenient means for the safe keeping of valuables.

Although every facility is afforded the box holder or the vault lessee for easy access to his or her property, its private examination and the transaction of business, no similar opportunity is possible to an unauthorized person.

During nearly fifty years' experience this Company has never had a loss of property intrusted to its care.

In order to secure the best vaults, the services of *The Hollar Company*, Engineers, Designers and Superintendents of Bank-Vault Construction, were retained for the purpose of making the plans and specifications; also to superintend the construction of the work in the factory and its erection in the building.

IMMENSE VAULTS

Ten Fire- and Burglar-Proof Vaults have been installed. Two of the largest of these vaults are for general safe-deposit purposes and are of the round door type. In selecting the material to be used in the construction of all the vaults, consideration was given to the physical properties of that metal which would offer the greatest resistance to penetration.

The vaults and doors are formed of layers of five-ply welded and hardened Chrome Steel and Iron and Open Hearth Steel in alternate layers, joined together in the strongest manner possible from the inside with threaded bolts of welded, twisted and hardened steel and iron. The door of the largest of the Safe-Deposit Vaults weighs over 16 tons and is grounded like a valve to an absolutely air-tight joint in order to preclude the introduction of liquid or other explosives.

The locking bolts of this door radiate from the center, after the manner of the spokes in a wheel, and are operated by a specially designed motor, which is in turn checked and controlled by an electrically winding time lock. All of this mechanism is controlled without connection or holes through the doors.

Should conditions arise, however, which would, in the opinion of the custodian of the vault, justify keeping the vault locked for any additional number of hours beyond the time for which it was originally set, this can be accomplished without opening the vault door, or without any one having access to the locks. The value of this feature will be appreciated when the contingency of fire or riot is considered, for in either case it would be undesirable to permit the unlocking

MAIN CORRIDOR LOOKING EAST
THE SAFE DEPOSIT COMPANY OF NEW YORK

of the vault, and all that would be necessary would be to close an electric switch, when the time lock would be electrically wound, thereby preventing the opening of the door until the expiration of the added number of hours.

The vaults are furnished with several thousand safe-deposit boxes of various sizes. Each box is provided with a combination lock or with one or more changeable combination key locks. The latter are so arranged that it requires the presence of the renter with his key and the custodian of the vault with a separate key to obtain entrance to the box. By the use of these key locks a degree of protection never before secured by the use of any key lock is

ENTRANCE TO SAFE DEPOSIT VAULT No. 1
THE SAFE DEPOSIT COMPANY OF NEW YORK

COUPON ROOMS LOOKING NORTH FROM EAST END OF MAIN CORRIDOR
THE SAFE DEPOSIT COMPANY OF NEW YORK

veniently furnished Coupon Rooms, and three large Committee Rooms; they are thoroughly lighted and ventilated and insure complete pri-

PRIVATE COUPON ROOMS vacy. Each room has its telephone connection, a convenient means of communication for the purchase and sale of securities or for such other purposes as may be desirable for the Company's patrons.

SPECIAL FACILITIES FOR LADIES Extending south from the Reading Room is a corridor leading to the Ladies' Department containing eight separate Coupon Rooms and all essential conveniences.

obtained. The difference between this changeable combination key lock and that of any other type of safe-deposit key lock is as great as the difference between an ordinary key and a combination safe lock.

Eight individual Security Vaults, each with separate anteroom, have been provided for individuals or corporations requiring more space and exclusiveness than may be had under other conditions.

All of the vaults have been amply provided with electrical protection; also with a separate watch system.

There is also ample room for the safe and convenient storage of valuables intrusted to the Company's care, such as plate, bullion, etc.

Adjoining the main vaults are twenty-six con-

INTERIOR OF SAFE DEPOSIT VAULT No. 1
THE SAFE DEPOSIT COMPANY OF NEW YORK

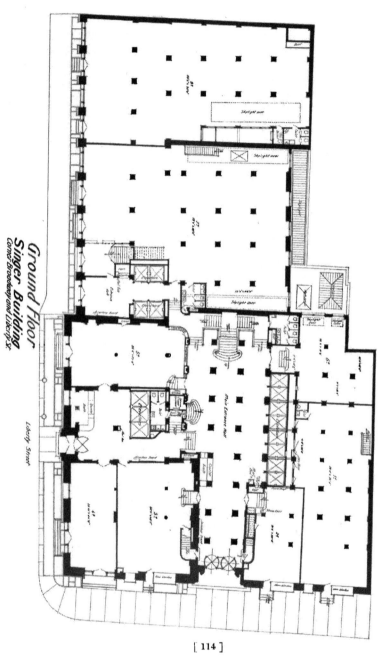

Ground Floor
Singer Building
Corner Broadway and Liberty St.

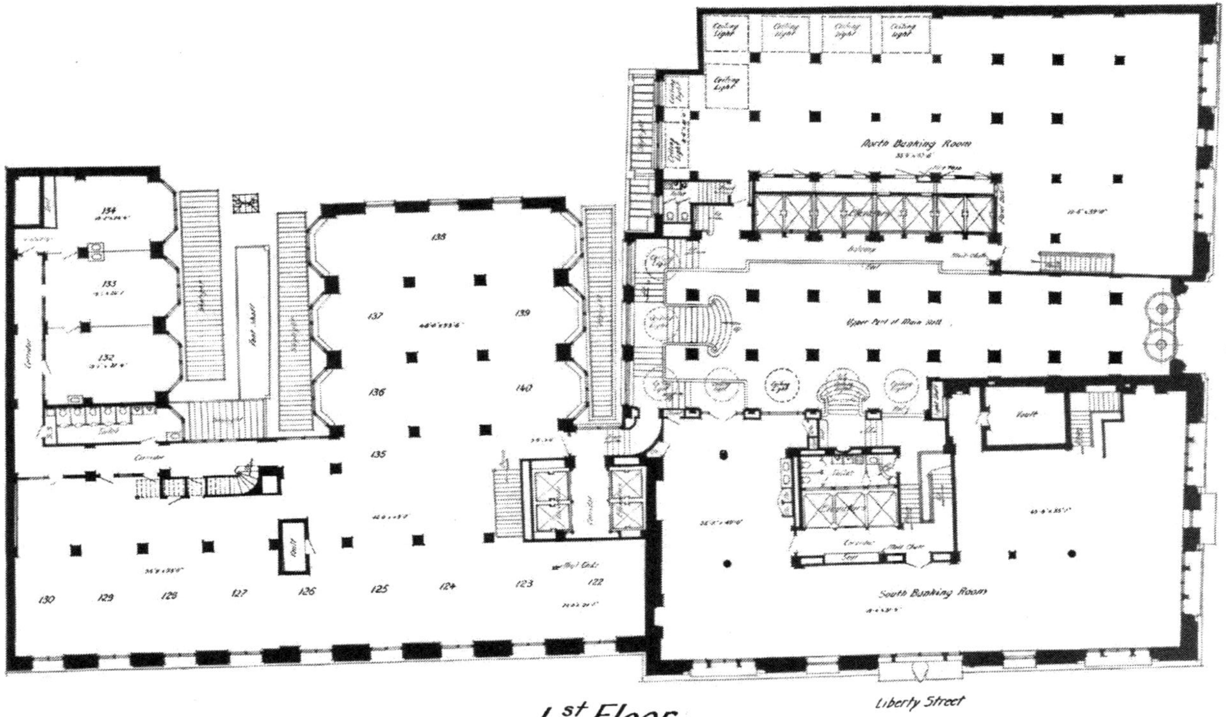

1st Floor

Singer Building
Corner Broadway and Liberty St.

Liberty Street

Broadway

[115]

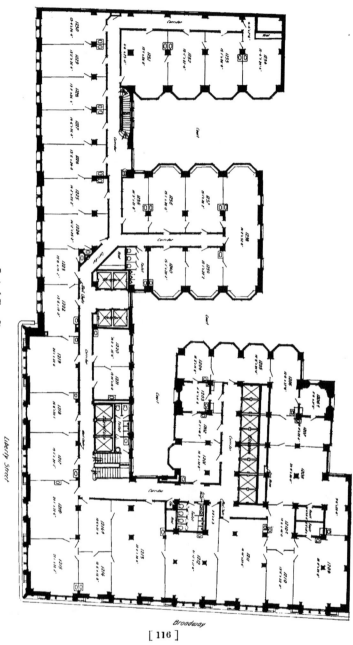

Typical Floor Plan
Singer Building
Corner Broadway and Liberty St.

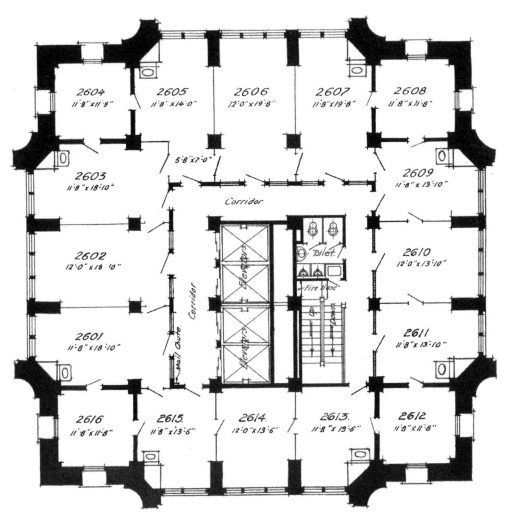

Typical Tower Floor Plan

Singer Building
Corner Broadway and Liberty St.